CAPACITY

Power Keys to Rising Up and Staying up!

David S. Philemon

Royal Diadem Publishing Inc.

*To the Almighty God, my Rock, Refuge, and Source of all wisdom
and strength. Thank You for Your unwavering love, grace, and the
purpose You've placed within me. May this book bring glory to
Your name and draw others closer to You.*

*And to my beloved spiritual parents, Dr. Paul and Dr. Mrs. Becky
Paul Enenche, who have faithfully nurtured and guided me
in this journey. Your example of unwavering devotion, godly
counsel, and compassionate care has been a beacon of light
and strength in my life. Thank you for standing as pillars of
faith and for your steadfast commitment to the Kingdom.*

ACKNOWLEDGMENTS

This book would not have been possible without the unwavering support, dedication, and talent of an extraordinary team. My deepest gratitude goes to each of you for your contributions, insights, and encouragement throughout this journey.

First and foremost, thank you to Rev. Mimi Philemon my dear wife, Rev. Shina Gentry, and and my assistant pastor Rev. Bright Amudoaghan for your incredible effort, encouragement, and belief in this project. Your support has been instrumental in bringing this vision to life.

To the dedicated leaders of Royal Diadem Publishing, Ide Imogie and Kishawna Bailey, I am immensely grateful for your belief in this project from the very beginning and for investing your time and energy into its development. Your creativity, dedication, and expertise have been the backbone of this endeavor.

I am especially grateful to the Royal Diadem Publishing team— Beulah Orogun, Emmanuella Ben-Eboh, Doyinsade Awodele, Kim Matthews, and Shante Gill, for your meticulous attention to detail, refining every page and ensuring that each word reflects our vision.

A heartfelt thank you to my family, friends, and colleagues whose unwavering support and belief in this project gave me the courage and strength to see it through.

Finally, thank you to all the readers and supporters who make this work meaningful. I am humbled and honored to share this journey with each of you.

With all my gratitude,
David Philemon

CONTENTS

APOSTLE DR. DAVID PHILEMON

INTRODUCTION

Activating Your Prophetic Promises

"**H**annah prayed and said, my heart exults and triumphs in the Lord; my horn (my strength) is lifted in the Lord. My mouth is no longer silent, for it is opened wide over my enemies because I rejoice in Your salvation." 1 Samuel 2:1 AMP

The King James says, "*My mouth is enlarged over my enemies.*"

Most of the time, no matter how hard certain people try to rise, they fail repeatedly. It's because either they have given the enemy so much power and credit, or they have taken the enemy for granted. Some give the enemy much power and credit: "Why couldn't you do it?" "The enemy stopped me." "Why are you where you are?" "The enemy is stopping me." "Why are things not working?" "The enemy is fighting me." This pattern of thinking, deeply ingrained in many believers, creates a self-fulfilling prophecy of defeat, where every setback is attributed to an omnipotent adversary, leaving no room for personal growth or divine intervention.

You're not the only one the enemy is fighting. There are enemies from the foundation of this Earth, of this world. Even God Almighty in Heaven above had, and still has an enemy, but that hasn't stopped Him from being God. God has never said, "I couldn't be God, and I'm not doing very well because the enemy is stopping me." If the Creator of the universe continues to reign supreme despite adversaries, how much more should we, as His children, rise above the challenges that confront us?

Also, no matter how hard they try, some can't rise and succeed because they take and keep taking the enemy for granted. This dangerous oversight stems from a misplaced sense of invulnerability, a belief that faith shields us from all harm without needing spiritual vigilance or preparation. Such complacency exposes you to the enemy's subtle yet devastating tactics, which exploits every opportunity to undermine their progress and diminish your impact on the world.

God can use enemies to make you greater, better, stronger, and more successful. At the same time, Satan can use enemies to shrink your life. More often than not, Satan uses his enemies not just to mock a person's life but to shrink the person's life. So when a person tries to go up, enemies show up, pulling the person down. This dynamic interplay between divine upliftment and satanic oppression creates a spiritual battlefield for every advancement to meet with resistance, every victory challenged by a counterattack. The key lies in discerning which forces work in our lives and aligning ourselves with God's purposes to overcome the enemy's strategies.

But as a child of God who understands the lifting power of the Father, you know that it doesn't matter how many enemies rise against you; they will always go down. This confidence in God's supremacy forms the bedrock of our spiritual resilience, enabling us to stand firm in the face of opposition, knowing that our ultimate victory is assured not by our strength but by the power of the One who calls us His own.

Many people have been overtaken by the enemy simply because, although they have God, they don't know how to connect with God, walk with God, or align with God to defeat their enemies. Every time the enemy launches an attack, they go down. The Israelites couldn't explain the mystery behind their stagnation, frustration, and failures.

The Bible says, *"None could lift his head. Zechariah 1:21:"* They didn't know why. In Zechariah 1:17, God prophesied, *"Through prosperity, my city shall yet spread abroad."* The prophet just prophesied that the Lord is bringing prosperity to the land. Everyone will prosper. Everyone will build houses. Everyone will succeed. And they were screaming, "Yes! Amen! They took the prophecy and went to bed, only to realize that all the powerful prophecies almost looked like a curse year after year. None of it had come to pass. Why? Because you war with prophecy, you don't watch prophecy.

This pattern of unfulfilled promises and dashed hopes is not unique to ancient Israel; it plagues many believers today who fail to understand their active role in bringing God's words to pass. Prophecy is not a spectator sport but a call to spiritual arms, requiring us to partner with God in manifesting His will on earth. The gap between prophetic declaration and practical realization often widens due to our passive approach to faith, where we expect God to do all the work while we simply wait and watch.

There are specific spiritual postures that you can take—either in your heart, mind or physically—that prophecies meant to take you up will begin to bring you down. The Lord Almighty declared that the cities of Israel would again overflow with prosperity, and they screamed, "Amen!" The Lord will again comfort Jerusalem, bless her, and live in her. Everybody screamed, "Amen!" They screamed, "Amen!" Just like you, only for them to relax, the next thing that happened because of the prophecy was that hell was provoked, and suddenly things looked down. This paradoxical outcome stems from a fundamental misunderstanding of spiritual principles, where blessings turn to curses and promises lead to setbacks. Our alignment or misalignment with God's purposes can amplify or nullify the power of prophetic words spoken over our lives.

Because you're a child of God, enemies can't do anything to you. But I want you to think again. You never assume victory; you ensure victory. When a believer fails to understand what it takes to be properly aligned with God, all the suffering and all the pain become useless because it will never make sense until you properly align with God. God is ready to empower you to align effectively so that every prophetic word spoken over your life, family, church, and generation will come to pass in the name of Jesus.

I want you to see this resource in your hand as a tool for your lifting. Your life is about to take a new turn that will cause a significant breakthrough for you and your family. The keys to a lifted life. Welcome to the principles of divine alignment and spiritual warfare, and prepare yourself for a radical shift in perspective that will unlock doors that are long closed and break chains that are long binding. The path to your prophetic promises lies not in passive waiting but in active engagement with the God who speaks them into existence.

CHAPTER ONE

WAR WITH PROPHESIES

There are certain things that God has ordained this generation to give birth to. Now it's up to you whether or not what God is birthing will be birthed through you, but what God is birthing will be birthed because there is an agenda and a calendar. The only challenge is: Is there a set man? Are there set of people who are more than willing to be properly aligned with God so that everything God wants to birth will be birthed?

Zechariah 1:18-19 TLB says, "Then I looked and saw four animal horns! 'What are these?' I asked the angel. He replied, 'They represent the four world powers that have scattered Judah, Israel, and Jerusalem.'"

The four horns represent power, nation, kingdom. They represent the world powers. So it doesn't matter who you are; there are powers from the north, south, east, and west that are already on automatic drive to see that anything God speaks concerning you fails. In this case, you are not giving credit to the enemy, yet you are not taking the enemy for granted. Horns don't just stop their meaning with power; they also mean authority, nations, kingdoms, thrones. Verse 19 AMP: "So I asked the angel who was speaking with me, 'What are these?' And he answered me, 'These are the horns, the powerful Gentile nations that have scattered Judah (the southern kingdom), Israel (the northern kingdom), and Jerusalem (the capital city of Judah).'"

Judah, Israel, Jerusalem—all of them—did not know why things weren't working. They were fighting each other. But you know, the worst kind of fight is the fight where you are now fighting yourself. They were fighting each other, but they didn't know what was going on. They didn't know that behind the fight were demonic entities—demonic powers that had vowed to scatter everything God wanted to do or was doing. And verse 20 TPT says, *"and the Lord showed me four craftsmen."* I asked, "What are these horns and craftsmen coming to do?" And he said, "These are the horns—powers—that have scattered Judah so that no man raised up his head because of the suffering inflicted by the horns."

You thought you didn't have a job. You thought you didn't have a certificate or couldn't attend school. You thought nobody liked you. And the worst of it—you blame everybody for not liking you. Now you yourself don't even like yourself, because the things you do to yourself show that you don't like yourself. And you thought it's just life happening, not knowing that behind the happenings are powers inflicting suffering on your mind, your body, your finances, your relationships. Even if Jesus comes down today and hugs you and takes you out for dinner, by tomorrow, you will break up with Jesus. Even if He comes down today and employs you, giving you a seven-figure job, within one week, you will fire yourself or you will fire Jesus! Because certain powers (forces) are behind your suffering.

They have inflicted suffering upon you. But He said, "These craftsmen have come to terrify them." That's why the worst thing you can do to yourself is to despise a ministry God sends to destroy the powers holding you down. Because if you were powerful, you could have destroyed those powers. In fact, in the first place, if you were powerful, those powers should not have been able to inflict suffering on you. What most of us don't understand is that God has worked on certain people, and there are specific strategies—specific spiritual techniques, specific divine ways—that men and women that have encountered God will help you in dealing with these demonic entities.

So, those internal suffering, mental suffering, emotional suffering, financial suffering, career suffering, destiny suffering—you have the potential of a nuclear warhead, yet you can't even light a match, and Satan is happy. Every time you try to raise your head up in honor, Satan knows he has kept your head down, and so he goes about whispering, screaming, shouting, and declaring that there's no help for you in God. Satan has more faith than many believers. Satan knows that because of what he has put together, you can never rise and become anything. That's why I'm teaching you this now so that you can navigate your way out.

But the worst of this kind of thing is for the deliverer to be more interested in your deliverance than the one that needs the deliverance. That's how you know that witchcraft is sitting on your head. This is a call to personal desperation. You must cry out and reject any and everything that has inflicted suffering on your life. Do you think it's expected that your mates are higher than you? You started that job together; now you're answering "sir" and "ma" because they left you behind. People who are rising don't rise by mistake, and those who fall don't fall by mistake. Oh no, it's not by mistake. To you, it's your mistake that has kept you stagnant, but go back and check behind the curtain.

There are powers that orchestrated your mistake. They pulled the string, and because of your powerlessness, you responded to the pull of those demonic strings. "God sent these craftsmen." I'm glad He said artisans because a craftsman has a craft, knows his craft, and uses a craft. Unfortunately many people, are used to witchcraft, but they don't know that to paralyze witchcraft, you need God-craft.

Exodus 7:10 AMP says, "So Moses and Aaron came to Pharaoh, and did just as the Lord had commanded; Aaron threw down his staff before Pharaoh and his servants, and it became a serpent."

Moses did not just enter Egypt as a prophet; he entered Egypt as a craftsman. The first thing he used in creating attention was a craft. He put the stick down, and the stick became a snake. "What is this?" they asked. They put theirs down, too. By the time all the God-craftsmen and the witchcraft-men showed up and everybody crafted their craft, the weaker craft became subject to the higher craft. You thought that your captivity was normal—430 years of bondage—and scripture said, "Moses, use the snake!" Thank God Moses was not as argumentative as many Christians are. "Moses, use the snake!" Moses could have said, "Ah no, God, how can we use a snake? You are a good God; you are a great God. A snake? No, if I use a snake, they would think I'm a witch!" Witch what? Witchcraft. It's a craft, yes! Use craft. Craft versus craft.

Many people fail because they lack artisans in their lives. There are no unbeliever kings who go out to fight without consulting their witchcraft, but Christians take their God-craft for granted. David never went out to fight on the assumption. "Lord, shall I go? Will you deliver yes or no?" God used mulberry trees to give David a sign—God-craft. You are not more spiritual than God. Four hundred years of captivity—they thought it was normal.

So Moses started the God-craft: sign number one, sign number two, sign number three, sign number four, and then sign number nine. And Moses asked, "God, where are we going with this?" And God said, *"I have a shocker." God said, "We have to do one more sign."* Exodus 12:23 AMP says, "For the Lord will pass through to strike the Egyptians; and when He sees the blood on the lintel and the two doorposts, the Lord will pass over the door and will not allow the destroyer to come into your houses to slay you." And you know what that one more sign was? God told Moses, *"This night, I will pass through Egypt. Why? I will judge the gods of the Egyptians."* What? So you mean that all of these years of captivity were not with open, clear eyes? That witchcraft was behind it all? As I am, with all grace and oil and anointing and everything that I have, do you know that it's by the grace of God I never step out a day without oil on my head? I am anointed, and I have my craft.

We have oil in my house. When my kids finish showering, before they leave the house to school, they have to pray and get oil and put oil on their heads. Start thinking evil towards me, and it doesn't have to manifest—the thought of it will backfire. And you say, "David Philemon is using something." Absolutely. God said, "I will pass through the land this night, and I will strike down all the firstborn in the land of Egypt, both man and animals. I will execute judgment against the gods of Egypt, exhibiting their worthlessness.

I am the Lord." When you take certain things for granted, you become a victim of witchcraft. The Bible says he saw these craftsmen and the angel said to him, "These craftsmen are here to do what?" These are the horns—the powers—that have scattered Judah so that no man raised up his head because of the suffering inflicted by the Gentile nations. But these craftsmen have come to terrify them. And we don't stop at panicking them—they make them panic and throw down the horns of the nations who have lifted up their horns against the land of Judah to scatter it.

The Mystery Of Horns

There is a height meant for you to occupy. So listen to what Hannah said. The Bible says horns came to scatter. Hannah was barren and couldn't have a baby, but one day, when she discovered certain spiritual mysteries, the baby came.

> *1 Samuel 2:1 AMP says: "Hannah prayed and said, 'My heart rejoices and triumphs in the Lord; My horn (strength) is lifted in the Lord, My mouth has opened wide [to speak boldly] against my enemies Because I rejoice in Your salvation.'"*

You triumph. When did she fight? I thought the time we heard about her, she cried on the altar. To triumph means I fought and I defeated the enemy without getting any scars, any wounds, or any bruises on me. So when did she fight? She realized that her life's barrenness resulted from certain horns—the horn of barrenness, the empire of barrenness. A satanic horn made her barren.

Sometimes I laugh at young girls who don't understand the

mystery behind satanic insult and harassment. My horn is exalted, which means my authority, my own power, my own dominion, my own throne, is lifted up in the Lord. He said, "Now that my horn is exalted, my mouth has opened wide." See, let me tell you, there is a correlation between the authority of audacity and your vocal proclamation. That's why you know you are truly dying when you become silent, and you can't talk.

Never, ever be silent or quiet when life is not going the way it ought to go. Fighting the wrong thing is foolishness. You are dealing with horns, and then you go and start fighting your father, fighting your mother, fighting your brother, fighting your sister. Some people foolishly fight their spiritual parents.

Saul was dealing with the horn of witchcraft from his grandmother's place. The one man God raised to help him overcome became the man he fought every time. Who is the stupid rebel? Are you? Who is the idiot? It's you. Who is the one who disobeys God? It's you. Who is the one interceding and pleading for your mercy? It's your prophet, your father. Who is the one you are fighting? The same man is praying for you. What level of demonic craft is that?

The man you should run to, call every day, and say, "Papa, I don't understand what's going on with me," became the man he was fighting. He was hating. He hated Samuel for no reason because Samuel told him, "God has been warning you." But every time, Saul just hated his spiritual father, the one man who could help him.

Samuel finished his work. Samuel checked out. Who was the one that ended up losing? The guy that did not receive deliverance. And guess what? He didn't receive deliverance; number one, his three sons died in his presence. Then he died, and he took his three sons. He took Jonathan—his only Jonathan is mentioned there—but by the time you look, it says he took Jonathan and the chiefs. Why? Saul took his sons with him to the witchcraft coven. And the Bible says Saul died not only because he committed one bad sin or the other. It says because he went to seek a witch because of his error. His sons died because he went to consult a witch. His sons died. Saul died.

Let me tell you, if you take the art of craft for granted, you will be grounded. Hannah said, "*I am now rejoicing.*" But Saul died. 1 Chronicles 10:13-14 AMP says: "*So Saul died for his trespass which he committed against the Lord, for his failure to keep the word of the Lord; and also because he consulted a medium [regarding a spirit of the dead] to inquire of her, and did not inquire of the Lord [instead]. Therefore, the Lord put him to death and turned the kingdom over to David, the son of Jesse.*"

Why is it that you are face to face with opportunity, and you are the one who uses your hand to destroy the opportunity? Then you go back and beat yourself, not knowing that a horn from behind the scenes manipulated you. "My mouth has opened wide to speak boldly against my enemies." Never, ever try to open your big mouth against your enemies until you know horn has been exalted. That's why many believers fail, because their horn has not been exalted yet they have big mouths against the enemy. So, by the time they finish screaming and attacking the enemy, they go to bed, and the enemy comes and deals with them.

> *The evil spirit said, "I know Paul, and I know Jesus,*
> *but who are you?" (Acts 19:15 NIV)*

There are crafts in the spirit realm. Moses used his craft to incapacitate the Egyptians. So what is your goal? Your goal is to labor to see that your horn is exalted constantly.

The Power Of Alignment

> *Psalm 92:10-11 KJV says: "But my horn shalt thou exalt like*
> *the horn of an unicorn: I shall be anointed with fresh oil. Mine*
> *eye also shall see my desire on mine enemies, and mine ears*
> *shall hear my desire of the wicked that rise against me."*

Hannah said, "My mouth is enlarged over my enemies. My mouth —I can speak with my mouth and bring down my enemies because my horn has been exalted. My horn has been exalted. My eyes also shall see my desire on my enemies, and my ears shall hear my desire of the wicked that rise up against me."

Many take for granted the rising of the wicked. So when the wicked rise against them, they bring them down. And you take it for granted. You don't give credit and power to the enemy, yet you don't take the enemy for granted. And yet, you don't leave yourself unprotected. Because if you leave yourself unprotected, your horn unexalted, the time comes, and you'll be like Samson: "I will arise, I will shake myself." And when they say, "Pray and scatter all the powers attacking you," yeah, but you are not correctly aligned. So by the time you open your mouth, you're announcing to the enemies that "I'm still here fighting," only for them to show up.

The Bible says when the Israelites took the Ark of the Covenant into the battlefield, there was a shout to the point the Philistines panicked. And they said, "Wow! That is the same Ark that defeated, opened the Red Sea, and killed many kings." Then the men said, "Hey, run away!" No, they said, "Quit yourselves as men. Equip yourselves as men and fight."

What's going on? 1 Samuel 4:6-9 TLB says: *"'What is all the shouting about over in the camp of the Hebrews?' the Philistines asked. They panicked when they were told it was because the Ark of the Lord had arrived. 'God has come into their camp!' they cried out. 'Woe upon us, for we have never faced anything like this. Who can save us from these mighty gods of Israel? They are the same gods who destroyed the Egyptians with plagues when Israel was in the wilderness. Fight as you never have before, O Philistines, or we will become their slaves just as they have been ours.'"*

Their enemies feared what God could do. So the Philistines fought desperately, and Israel was defeated again. What happened? The Ark came, and you still failed? If only you will give me water, if only you will provide me with oil, if only you will lay hands and lay leg, all my witchcraft battles will be over! It's not true! If your heart is not exalted, if your heart is not rejoicing in the Lord, you will never enjoy what the Lord can do. Spiritual things are not magical; you have to be aligned.

"My heart rejoices in the Lord."

There has to be a heart alignment. The Israelites were defeated again. What happened? The Bible says, to make matters worse, by the time they were defeated, the Philistines now took the Ark—the same Ark they feared. They took it. The Bible says when they got back and told the wife of Phinehas, "Your husband and his brother are dead because they thought they could be careless with God and win over the enemy," Oh, by the way, "Madam, the Ark has been taken." The woman screamed, and she said, "Ichabod, the glory has departed." She gave birth to a baby called Ichabod—"The glory has departed."

That day, Eli fell down, broke his neck, and died. If they had not gone out to fight those witchcraft battles, their lives would have been better. But if you don't fight, you remain a slave. Now, if you want to fight, you must decide that you will not be the loser. And it's so easy to lose when you assume victory. You stay with God. The Ark couldn't save them. When they took that same Ark into the house of Dagon, with no assistance, the Ark beat down Dagon —to let you know, "I still have power." The only thing is that my power won't work for an idiot.

The enemy is desperately eager to defeat you, and God is anxious to help you and make it impossible for the enemy to beat you. So God will lift you up, and the call to you right now is a call of the heart. He said, "My heart rejoiceth in the Lord. My mouth is enlarged over my enemies."

Before you open your mouth, make sure you correct your heart. God knows that enemies will seek ways to bring you down, so He said concerning David, "The enemy will not exact upon him, nor the sons of wickedness afflict him." (Psalm 89:22 KJV)

CHAPTER TWO

THREE-FOLD ASSIGNMENT

Correction Of The Heart

T he biggest disease in the body of Christ is a heart disease. you can be talking with somebody, and they are imagining evil towards you. they are looking for ways just to bring you down. it's a heart issue—wickedness in the hearts of men, evil in the hearts of men, witchcraft in the hearts of men. although Satan thought he had infiltrated the body of Christ with a deep level of wickedness and witchcraft, god still has certain people, and I want you to make yourself one of those people.

what did god say about Saul? he said Saul was an evil man. what did god say about David? his heart is after my heart. it was a heart issue. a man after god's own heart.

I want you to deal with that matter today because the bible says in the last days, men's hearts will fail. Men's hearts will fail. why? because of the abundance of iniquity, wickedness. All that Saul did was to pray. all that samuel did was to pray for Saul. all that Saul did was to hate samuel. look at this man who couldn't even go to see the prophet without an offering—now, he had become a "big boy." and so, even to see the prophet, even to serve god, to allow the prophet to tell god that Saul will kill me if he sees me doing your will...

Matthew 27:4 amp says: "saying, 'i have sinned by betraying innocent
blood.' but they said, 'what is that to us? see to that yourself!'"

Judas Iscariot was allowed by Jesus for three and a half years. So when god allows particular evil in a specific environment, he allows that evil to change, right? But then, the only thing is that the wickedness of the wicked keeps taking them deeper and deeper and deeper until one day, judas doesn't even know that he has already swallowed what he can no longer forfeit. He went and looked at him—he killed himself.

The bad thing with many people is that they will fall in love with Pharisees who have no plan for their lives. They don't care about you. People who don't even care about you, people who don't even care about your future, and those who don't care about your dreams become the ones that you're loyal to. Why? Because you have that evil agenda.

The same Jesus that gave you a position, even though you've been stealing for three and a half years, is the one you go and sell for the price of an enslaved person. As soon as Judas returned to the Pharisees, he said, "No, no, no, I don't like it. Take your money. This business is not a good one." they showed him their true colors. The Bible says they looked at him and rebuked him. They said, "What have we to do with you?" they looked at him, saying, "I have sinned by betraying innocent blood." they replied, "What is that to us? see to that yourself—that's your business!" "What is that to us?" why is it that people will be more committed to that which will destroy them and to those who hate them and are killing them than to those who genuinely care? Can i tell you why? It's because the heart of such an individual is evil.

To the crooked, you will show yourself crooked. If you find it difficult to be loyal to those genuinely committed to your destiny, the problem is a heart problem. You have a problem with your heart. And if god works on that heart—if you allow him to work on that heart—you will be shocked at how easy it is to be free from crooked people. You will be bold enough to stand up for what is right. You will be bold. With the pure, you show yourself pure, and with the crooked, you show yourself crooked. That doesn't mean god is crooked—you show yourself as god.

Alignment Of Heart

I don't care where the enemy puts you. If you allow God to correct your heart, I'm telling you, you will be supernaturally elevated. Sometimes, the correction of your heart does not mean that you are evil towards anybody, but it means that your heart has now shifted in trust from god, and you are putting your trust in people. Because if you put your trust in people, they will hurt and disappoint you. That was what happened to Joseph. God left him two extra years in jail because he was now trusting the man who interpreted his dream.

Let God use you—do whatever he wants to do. Don't tell God where he should bless you—just give him that option. Sometimes, you'll be shocked that when God decides to turn his face and bless you, he will use lepers as your helpers. God can use lepers to do what all those strong people cannot do if your heart is right. Do you understand? God is God.

Joseph's mistake was to tell that man, "Remember me. When you get to Pharaoh, tell him I was wrongly put here. I was wrongly accused. I was innocent." And when the guy got there, he forgot. So in the writing of Josephus, the historian of Jewish history, he was able to bring that picture clearer and said, "God, the God of Israel, allowed Joseph to remain in that place for two extra years until Joseph repented, literally, and got his heart right." You can find some of that in Joseph's prayers—he repented and said, "god, have mercy on me, that I have always put my trust in you, but now I put my trust in man."

When he started praying a few months later, Pharaoh had a dream. The man who forgot him remembered him. If god will lift you, let him decide how he will lift you. All you need is a right heart, and I can kneel here and tell you, your heart can't be correct, and the earth not to lift you high. God can't be exalted in your heart, and you are demoted on the planet. It's impossible. The justice of god rejects that. A widow can't honor the voice of god through a prophet and ends up in lack and want. It's impossible. Nobody ever stands up for the kingdom, rescuing the kingdom of god, and is a disgrace. It's impossible.

If you think your heart is right, people will ride over you—no! God will not let them ride over you. And even when they think they're riding over you, they don't know you are riding them to your destiny. When a good man's heart becomes dirty, Satan travels through that dirt to make the man's life dirty. All through the mistakes of David, god never did anything wrong. Even when David did wrong, god came to David. He said, "If you needed women, I would have given you many. Why must you take this one and kill the man?" so none of the things David did mess up his destiny, like the fact that his heart shifted from being a pure, good, clean heart.

If it is easy for demons to always come to you—can you see how fast they come?—every time they come to a place in your life, those things don't have a day when they arrive. My life just evolves. I want to correct my heart. Witchcraft has never, ever been known to be more potent than god-craft. Witchcraft is when Satan, through his dark powers and dark ways, releases wickedness toward people, either as a way of proving his point or as a way of revenge against people. Satan releases wickedness toward people using witchcraft. Usually, it results in so many ugly things. One of the things that the wickedness of Satan does to people is to keep them in spiritual bondage.

Spiritual bondage is when a person's spirit is arrested by evil spirits, oppressed by foul spirits, harassed by dark spirits, and tortured by dark powers. Witchcraft always results in spiritual oppression. It is when Satan uses his dark powers and dark means to arrest a person spiritually, incapacitating them or making it difficult for them to either initiate their deliverance or connect with their deliverer. Witchcraft is so wicked that it never feels sorry or pity for the one it is bewitching. It transfers the bewitchment to the next generation and spreads the bewitchment like cancer, among others. So if no one can either initiate their deliverance or connect with their deliverer, witchcraft never leaves a family.

Spiritual oppression may not be a direct result of witchcraft, but witchcraft activity will always result in spiritual oppression. Spiritual oppression includes being a victim of spiritual bondage. Many people are tortured and tormented by evil spirits. The Bible says because of the rebellion of Saul, the spirit of god left him. So, guess why Saul rebelled? Witchcraft. Witchcraft manipulation played a significant role and allowed Saul to want the throne God gave him, but he tried to deny the god that gave him the throne and hated the principles and procedures of the god who gave him the throne.

Witchcraft made him stubborn. No matter what Samuel preached to him, he never bowed. Sometimes, you see Christians, and they are proud to say, "There's nobody that can talk to me. I am me, myself." That means you are nobody! You are actually under witchcraft oppression. In every man's life, there ought to be somebody you fear, reverence, and respect. Otherwise, you can't go far no matter how hard you work. It's not prideful to say, "Nobody can talk to me. I am me in my world. nobody!" Sorry, it's not a thing of pride—it's just an expression of foolishness and arrogance that is the result of a witchcraft attack. Satan played that role in the life of Saul until one day, the man of god came and told him, "Saul, why are you doing this?" and Saul said, "It's because I want to sacrifice to god." The man of god said, "You don't know god. Obedience is better than sacrifice, to hearken than the fat of rams."

1 Samuel 15:23 NIV says: "For rebellion is like the sin of divination, and arrogance like the evil of idolatry. Because you have rejected the lord's word, he has rejected you as king."

Rebellion is the sin of witchcraft. When rebellion grows in your heart, it is as severe as the sin of divination, fortune-telling, and disobedience—as severe as false religion and idolatry. Because you have rejected the lord's word, he also has rejected you as king.

How do you know you are under witchcraft attack, under divination of hell?

It's when your heart keeps rejecting the word of the lord. You are still in church and hearing the word of the lord, but you are fighting the word of the lord, so the word of the lord can no longer work on you or change you. Why? You are under a witchcraft attack. In such a case, what should you do? Either initiate, appreciate your deliverance, go to god and say, "god, deliver me from witchcraft," or press into a god and receive deliverance. You can ask those who are walking with god to pray for you. Never, ever allow the seed of rebellion to grow in your heart.

"refusing to obey is as bad as the sin of sorcery."

Being stubborn and doing what you want is like the sin of worshiping idols. You refused to obey the lord's command, so he refused to accept you as king. The bible says the spirit of god left Saul, and when the spirit of god left Saul—because it's impossible for the human body not to be occupied by a spirit—the next chapter says the lord's spirit left Saul. It is not that the lord sent the evil spirit to the Soul. The word "sent" means permitted. So, instead of god protecting Saul's spirit from craft infiltration, the spirit of god left, and another spirit took over.

The lord permitted an evil spirit to torment Saul. And what did it cause him? Much trouble.

1 Samuel 16:14-15 MSG says: "At that very moment, the spirit of god left Saul. In its place, a black mood, sent by god, settled on him. he was terrified. Saul's advisors said, 'This awful tormenting depression from god is making your life miserable. Oh, master, let us help. Let us look for someone who can play the harp. When the black mood from god moves in, he will play his music, and you will feel better.'"

And what happened? "Saul told his servant, 'Go ahead, find me someone who can play well and bring him to me.'" And who did they find? David.

When they brought David, he began to play, and the scripture says that every time David played, the evil spirit lifted off Saul. Whenever that lousy depression from God tormented Saul, David got out his harp and played, and it would calm Saul down, and he would feel better as the mood lifted.

Before you know it, there was another battle; things happened, but guess what? The next thing Saul wanted to do was to take a spear to kill the only boy who was removing the evil spirit from him. That's how you know you are under a severe witchcraft attack—when you begin to find fault with your deliverer, attacking your deliverer. You can't initiate your deliverance yourself, yet god brought you help, and you're attacking your deliverer. That is it!

Many people, unfortunately, are victims of sorcery, and because some of them have exposed themselves to false prophets and have exposed themselves to palm readers—if you have ever exposed yourself to palm readers or someone in your family has consulted witch doctors, native doctors—the possibility of witchcraft spirits challenging and attacking you is high. If you have a great destiny, the chance of witchcraft attacking you is high.

What are you supposed to do? You are to make sure you stay away from that which will give witchcraft power to bring you down. Pride is one of those things. Wickedness is one of those things. In the case of David, he would play the harp, and Saul's mood would change. So, the harp was David's craft to defeat witchcraft. David had a harp-craft.

When witchcraft is at work, the following accompany him:

- SPIRITUAL OPPRESSION
- PHYSICAL BONDAGE
- FINANCIAL BONDAGE—MYSTERIOUS, INEXPLICABLE FINANCIAL DIFFICULTY

When Satan releases witchcraft, either as a point of punishment, vengeance, revenge, or as a way of proving a point, it usually results in a stagnant life or a life of constant, repeated negative cycles. You notice that is very visible is a continual demotion. People are not just stagnant; they are demoted. When I say demotion, I mean non-achievement.

Release Of Power For Personal And Family Elevation

Take this or leave it: If your mates, colleagues, and contemporaries are always ahead, you're under attack. Yes, there are times that God keeps you in a place for a season to work on you, to finish working on you, but that season—within that season—you will see the visible providential power of God. You will see some things God uses to prove to you, "I am with you, and I'm helping you." But that season has never been intended to be a long season. Never. We saw David's oppression, battles, and challenges in 13 years. The whole of Joseph's challenges—13 years. But believe me, within those 13 years, it's not like it was all 13 years of misery. Because within those 13 years, David was the man. He was so "Davidic" that the king's daughter loved him. Two of the king's daughters were in love with him, but Saul took one and gave it to someone else. David was mad! And Saul said, "Okay, I will compensate you."

Because when David was mad, David said, "Look, man, I know I'm young; you can't do that to me." Then the Bible says Saul was told that his other daughter, Michal, was in love with David. You know, that's the craziest part of it—she was in love with David, and yet she was the only woman who died barren in the Bible. Her passion was useless because she was not submitted to the Spirit that controls that man. If you despise the oil on a man, it will fight you. She loved him to the point that she allowed jealousy to make her undermine his purpose and his calling. She died barren.

Why didn't that love translate into greatness? And yet another woman who was a latecomer, who came from Bathsheba—she also loved David. She not only gave David a son but gave him a son who became the king. So, Michal's love for David wasn't enough because her heart was not aligned with David's calling. But Bathsheba submitted to David's spirit, and God blessed her.

Bathsheba's family had their own challenges and witchcraft battles because she was also the granddaughter of Ahithophel. In Saul's family, they had witchcraft. Saul's daughter Michal was Saul's daughter, but Bathsheba chose to submit to the prophet Nathan. The witchcraft in her family died. It failed. Her grandfather, who committed suicide for partnering with Absalom to torment King David, failed.

Witchcraft should have stopped Bathsheba's destiny, but guess what? She submitted to the prophet, and the prophet was God's craftsman. And every time this young lady yielded to the voice of the God-craftsman, her destiny shifted and got closer and closer. Witchcraft power could not stop her destiny. Some of us don't know that the things you are dealing with are 300 years older than you. How many years was it between the year that Rachel died and the time Saul became king? You are looking at something that was almost a thousand years old. But the spirit of witchcraft tracked Saul. The witchcraft was so wicked that it kept inviting Saul to danger and destruction. That's why witchcraft works through rebellion.

Saul didn't just become rebellious by accident. Witchcraft entered him through the sins of his ancestors. He became stubborn, unteachable, and disobedient, leading him to consult a witch. The rebellion was so deep that even when God gave Saul instructions through Samuel, he twisted and disobeyed. He wanted to do things his way, and that was witchcraft manipulating his heart.

Let me tell you, rebellion is one of the most incredible doors to witchcraft. Some people do not understand that when you are rebellious toward God's word or His servants, you open yourself up to witchcraft influence. Bathsheba had witchcraft influences in her family, too, but she aligned herself with God, submitted to His ways, and was elevated. Despite the adversities surrounding her, she gave birth to Solomon, the greatest king.

There are powers in every family that keep trying to bring people down, but if you align yourself with God, no witchcraft can stop you. You have to fight the powers behind your suffering. These powers might have existed for generations, but they will be destroyed when you understand the mysteries of God's craft. If you stay aligned with God, the powers of darkness will fail.

Some people don't understand that the reasons for their suffering go beyond physical issues. There are ancient powers, like the horns mentioned in Zechariah, representing demonic forces that have been fighting families for generations. But God always sends craftsmen—spiritual agents equipped to destroy those powers.

Do you know that your breakthrough might be waiting on your heart's alignment? You might be trying to fight battles in the physical realm, but God is telling you, "Align your heart with Me, and I will send My craftsmen to destroy the demonic forces fighting your life." That's what Bathsheba did. She aligned her heart with God, and God broke the cycle of witchcraft that was attacking her family. You see, it doesn't matter where you come from. It doesn't matter what kind of witchcraft or powers have been ruling over your family for hundreds of years. Once you align yourself with God, you will break free. She submitted and was under Nathan. Meanwhile Saul's daughter Michal, even though God gave her David as her prophet. Just so you know in the days of Michal, there was Nathan and Gad. But she still fought to see Saul. He thought he was being stubborn not knowing he was being invited by wicked spirit.

God has the power to lift you up especially above the power of the enemy. God's power reaching out and working on you until He begins to gives you personal grace to overcome your personal struggles, to turn failure into success, to give you supernatural ability to go through your toughest seasons of your life. That spirit didn't attack anyone in the family of Saul until someone became significant. He gives you the ability to embrace the necessary pain to obtain the needed heights.

Psalm 30:1-2 (TPT): *"I will exalt you, Yahweh, for you lifted me. You made me stand in a place of safety. You healed me. I cried out to you, Yahweh, and you restored my health."*

When he was going through the gloating enemies, it was a pain that needed God's healing power. There are things that happened that are worse than sickness. When you are lied against, when the people you are helping become the people hurting you.

1 Samuel 22:1 (MSG): *"David got away and escaped to the Cave of Adullam. When his brothers and others in his father's family heard where he was, they went down to join him."*

So when you look at luck, and it looks luck(less), they tried everything they could, and David became their leader. When the Amalekites came and took their wives, the first thing they said is they will kill David. They wanted to kill the man who changed their luck, who turned them from losers to champions, without thinking twice. Thank God He intervened.

You can say yes, I have forgiven you, but that won't stop me from saying, "I know who you are." Do you understand the kind of pain and grace it takes to maintain? David said God, you need to heal my heart because if I go about telling you how I feel. So, I don't want to torture you with guilt. I can bring you up and give you a position, but that doesn't mean that I won't forget you tried to kill me.

God releases his power to enable you to come out the deep places of sorrow. Because if you go through this in life, the things you go through can constantly seek to keep you down because Satan's agenda is that you keep sinking and sinking. Sorrow is a place of mess. Don't let me sink.

It doesn't matter what happened in the past now is the season of favor he is bring you out of the valley of despair. When God lifts you, he releases the power to sustain you at top so whatever the enemy does to see you turn down he turns the work of the enemy into a stool.

CHAPTER THREE

SUSTAINING YOUR LIFTING

Sustaining your lifting demands your utmost attention and understanding. Looking at the passion translation of Psalm 125:1 (TPT): "Those who trust in the Lord are as unshakeable, as unmovable as mighty Mount Zion! Just as the mountains surround Jerusalem, so the Lord's wrap-around presence surrounds His people, protecting them now and forever." When God lifts you, He's not just giving you a momentary boost, but He's stabilizing your entire life, making you as solid and unmovable as a mountain. This divine act of elevation isn't just about changing your circumstances; it's about fundamentally altering your spiritual DNA, infusing you with a stability that you need to stand strong for God.

However, this incredible gift of stability comes with a weighty responsibility. When God lifts and stabilizes your life, you must be vigilant, never allowing those things that sink men into your life. There are catalysts in this world – some that lift and others that drag people down. Developing a keen spiritual discernment to differentiate between these influences is crucial, guarding fiercely against anything that might erode the stability God has graciously bestowed upon you.

One of the most potent ways to maintain this elevated state is through an earnest, passionate study of God's nature. This isn't just an academic exercise but a heartfelt quest to understand what keeps God close to us and what causes Him to withdraw His presence. It's about developing a spiritual sensitivity so acute that we can align every facet of our lives with His will and character. We must seek what pleases and irritates Him, fine-tuning our spirits to resonate with His heart.

When we approach God with wide-open – hearts that are receptive, teachable, and ravenously hungry for divine wisdom – He never fails to respond. He becomes our master instructor, unwavering guide, and North Star in the tumultuous sea of life. His instructions become the scaffolding that enables us to stand tall amidst life's fiercest storms. The radiance of His countenance upon us isn't just a poetic metaphor; it's a tangible reality that solidifies our spiritual stance, making us as unshakeable as the ancient mountains themselves.

The promise is clear: when God's face shines upon an individual, His glory makes that person as solid as a mountain. You are lifted, never to sink. This divine elevation is meant to be permanent, a new state that redefines your existence. But what happens when it seems God has turned His face away? This question leads us to explore the depths of God's character and His working methods in our lives.

Psalm 113:8 in The Passion Translation gives us a glimpse into God's operation mode: "He promotes the poor, picking them up from the dirt, and rescues the needy from the garbage dump. He turns paupers into princes and seats them on their royal thrones of honor." Things start to change dramatically when He begins to work in a life. God's grace is a powerful force that provides in ways we can scarcely imagine. None of our poverty, failures, or glaring inadequacies intimidate or deter the Almighty. On the contrary, they become the raw materials from which He crafts the most extraordinary testimonies.

God delights in taking those at the bottom and elevating them to positions of honor and influence. He wants to make you a testimony He can share, a living, breathing example of His transformative power. No matter how dire they may seem, your current circumstances are not intimidating to God. He sees beyond your struggles to the glorious future He has planned for you.

However, we must confront a sobering reality: many don't last at the top because they forget where God picked them from. This spiritual amnesia is perhaps one of the greatest threats to our continued elevation and stability. It's all too easy to become complacent, to forget our desperate need for God's sustaining grace once we've tasted success. We must guard against this tendency with every fiber of our being, constantly reminding ourselves of the pit from which God has drawn us.

The journey of spiritual elevation often involves a process of divine exposure – a holy unveiling that can be both exhilarating and terrifying in equal measure. Wait until God begins to expose the actual condition of your heart; you may be shocked at how filthy it is. This exposure isn't meant to shame us but to bring us to a place of genuine humility and complete dependence on God. It's easy to think highly of ourselves when operating within the comfortable confines of our self-imposed limitations, but God sees beyond our facades to the core of who we are.

It's sobering to think that there are people whom God has not even placed where He ultimately wants them, yet they've already forgotten Him. Pride can creep in so subtly, hardening our hearts to the gentle whispers of the Holy Spirit. We must be vigilant against this insidious enemy of our souls, constantly checking our hearts for any signs of arrogance or self-sufficiency.

1 Peter 5:6-7 (ERV): *"So be humble under God's powerful hand. Then, he will lift you when the right time comes. Give all your worries to him because he cares for you."* This is the paradoxical nature of God's kingdom – the way up is down. Humility is the key that unlocks the door to sustained elevation. But this posture of humility isn't passive; it's accompanied by a call to "resist with vigor." We must understand how the devil attacks us, recognize his strategies, and stand firm against them.

It's crucial to understand that God doesn't turn His face from people because they are great; He turns His face from people because they are proud. The very hand that lifts us has the power to press us down if we become arrogant and self-sufficient. Many have not even entered the fullness of their rise, but they have already become full of themselves. This premature pride is a dangerous trap that we must vigilantly guard against.

James 4:7 KJV: "God will resist the proud but gives grace to the humble." If we don't submit to God, we can't hope to stand up to the evil that assails us. Keeping your heart pure and eradicating doubt is essential, for God's grace provides and sustains you.

Some people, in their spiritual journey, don't realize when they transition from being God's craftsmanship to becoming Satan's handiwork. When the heart is not pure, Satan can bring darkness to it, clouding our judgment and leading us astray. But a pure heart is like an impenetrable fortress – no matter what life throws at it, it remains undefeated. Show me a person with a pure heart, and I'll show you someone who cannot be ultimately defeated, regardless of circumstances.

It's important to note that not every son can connect with all the mantles of his spiritual father. This speaks to the uniqueness of each individual's calling and the specific gifts God has entrusted to them. We must be content with the particular mantle God has given us, not coveting the gifts or callings of others.

Some testimonies are so powerful, so otherworldly, that sharing them might be counterproductive or even dangerous. These are the deep, personal encounters with God's craftsmanship in our lives—moments of divine intervention and supernatural provision that defy human explanation. We must steward these experiences wisely, sharing them only as the Holy Spirit directs.

Even in times of apparent harassment or opposition, you must recognize that what Satan intends for evil, God can use for our greater good. The trials designed to break us often train us for something far beyond our comprehension. Satan may think he's harassing you, but he has no idea he's preparing you for something greater than he can handle.

Our opposition is often insignificant in the grand scheme – like crickets and king flies among eagles. What seems monumental in one realm becomes utterly irrelevant in higher spheres of spiritual authority. As you grow in this spiritual journey, you'll find yourself in positions of influence, sitting with high-power players who seek your counsel. This isn't a cause for pride but a humbling responsibility to steward the wisdom and discernment God has granted us.

You must develop spiritual discernment that allows you to see beyond surface appearances. When evil people stand before you and both smile, you see beyond the facade. The difference between you and them is that you're immunized against their influence. This spiritual immunity is a precious gift, allowing us to navigate treacherous waters without being contaminated by the evil around us.

Power of Surrender

One of the most significant prayers you can ever utter, and more importantly, cooperate with God as He begins to answer, is the simple yet profound request: "Lord, have Your way in me." It's easy for folks to claim that God owns their hearts, but let's be honest here - God doesn't truly own you if He can't have His way in you. It's like saying you've handed over the keys to your house but still dictating which rooms the new owner can enter. That isn't how it works with God, folks.

Let me tell you about this mission trip I just returned from - words can't do justice to the impact and the mighty works of the Lord I witnessed. Even if I had 100 days to describe it all to you, I couldn't capture the fullness of what went down. It was something else entirely. We didn't just travel to a place; we traveled in the glory, with the glory, and the glory accomplished things. Every aspect of our journey was drenched in God's presence, highly God-glorifying in ways that'll make your head spin.

A small boy, standing before a king and all his men, addresses them with heaven's wisdom. These weren't ordinary folks, mind you. We're talking about royalty and their entourage, sitting there for hours, hanging on every word. plenty of people have been coming to this place for years, trying to make a difference. But the news that spread like wildfire was that while others had been showing them how to do things, we brought light. That's a whole different ballgame, folks.

As all this was unfolding, I kept asking God, "Okay, what's the deal here? What's happening? What's next?" And let me tell you, the answer I got was something else. The Lord told me, "It's because you allowed Me to have My way. Your sacrifice was high, but your yieldedness was something else entirely." Can you wrap your head around that? It wasn't just about what we gave up; it was about how completely we surrendered to His will.

But hold onto your hats, because that wasn't even the kicker. The Lord continued, "You haven't seen anything yet. You will do more with My glory than with money." Now, that's a statement that'll make you sit up and take notice. We're so used to thinking we need fat wallets to make things happen for God, but He's saying there's a higher currency in His kingdom - His glory. When we tap into that, we're dealing with resources that make our bank accounts look like chump change.

The reception we got in Jos - man, it was something else. We're talking royal treatment, kind hospitality, elegance dripping from every corner. If we had to foot the bill for something like that, we'd be looking at numbers that'd make your eyes water. we didn't pay a dime. The Lord provided it all, just like that. And He didn't stop there. He made me a promise that'll knock your socks off: "I will never ever allow you and those that follow you to see shame or be shamed." That's not just a pat on the back; that's a divine guarantee, folks.

He looked at our sacrifice and said it wasn't just commendable; it was admirable. But then He dropped a bombshell: "What I'm about to do can only be done by My glory." That's when you know you're in for something big. We're talking about stuff that goes beyond human capability, beyond what money can buy or influence can achieve.

Here's where it gets really interesting. In the midst of us facing our own challenges, God throws us a curveball. He points to a community that's been struggling for over 100 years, having to travel 45 minutes to an hour just to fetch drinking water. And what does God say? "Give them water, I will burn it for you." Now, if that doesn't sound like God's sense of humor, I don't know what does. Here we are, dealing with our own issues, and God's telling us to solve someone else's problem that's been around for a century.

But that's how God operates, folks. He often tells you to do the seemingly senseless things in the sight of men. Why? Because He's watching to see where you put your trust. Is it in God or in your problems? This is where the rubber meets the road in our faith walk. You see, most folks find it hard to serve God the way He wants to be served because they've got another master. They're worshipping their problems, their battles, their challenges. Some of y'all are unknowingly worshipping your fears - the fear of the unknown. You're bowing down to these things, and that's why you find it difficult to make the necessary sacrifices God's asking for.

During this trip, I can't even tell you how many hours of sleep I got. It wasn't much, I can tell you that. We're talking heavy sun, the kind that makes you feel like you're being baked alive. But here's the kicker - instead of feeling worn out and beat down, I found myself feeling younger, fresher, and stronger. The Lord said to me, "I'm rewarding you with youthfulness." Now, that's something you won't find in your average health and wellness seminar, folks.

When you say, "Lord, I give You my heart. Lord, have Your way in me," do you really understand what you're saying? Let me break it down for you. You're essentially declaring this: there's nothing I have that's mine; there's nothing I am that's me. Everything I have, everything I am, and whatever I will become is all about You, God. That's heavy stuff, folks. It's not for the faint of heart. When you're faithful in little, God doesn't give you less work. He gives you grace to work more. So if you find that the work is becoming less, it's a sign of unfaithfulness or spiritual retirement. God's not in the business of downsizing His kingdom operations, folks.

Sometimes, you might miss certain things God wants to do with you. That's when God gives you another opportunity to go out of your way and connect with someone who's on course with Him. God's expecting to see you go the extra, extra mile to be a reproach remover. What He wants to do with your life is beyond your wildest dreams. He's been working on you, and I'm reminded of Joseph. After all the troubles and trials he went through, he was able to look at his brothers who sold him into slavery and say, "Don't worry, you didn't do it, God was behind it" (Genesis 50:20 ERV). That's the kind of perspective God wants you to have.

God wants you to constantly see Him behind everything, even what appears to be the devil at work. You need to understand that even the devil bows down to the purpose of God. So you can't sit there feeling sorry for yourself. The reason why it seems like you don't feel big on the inside is because you haven't yet connected to big stuff or with something bigger than you.

If you surrender, you have no idea what God has in mind. You have no idea what God will do with your life in your lifetime. God will use your life as a pen to sign the document of time and eternity. That's not just fancy talk; that's the reality of what happens when you fully yield to God's purpose.

Do you know what God really wants from you? He just wants channels. He wants partners - people that recognize His kingdom. Heaven and earth will pass away, but not a jot of His word will fall to the ground. In other words, what He intends to do will be done with or without you. But here's the kicker - what He intends to do will be better done with you. That's the privilege we have, folks. We get to be co-laborers with the Almighty God.

The Lord told me something that'll make you think. He said, "I don't want to use fishes to supply the needs of My kingdom." Why? When you finish taking the money from the fish, what do you do? You throw it in the pot of soup, make fish soup, grill it, eat it, or give it to someone else, and that's it. The life cycle of a fish is over.

God's looking for something more enduring, more impactful. He also said, "I don't prefer to use stones to worship Me." Think about it - if stones praise God, how will God reward them? Who will bless God for blessing stones? Who in the family of stones is it? The gravels? The dust? The sand? Who in the family of stones will begin to say, "This is the Lord's doing; it is marvelous in our sight"?

Only in the human family can God pick a pebble and turn it into a mountain, and people will look and say, "*No, this is the Lord's doing; it is marvelous in our sight.*" The earth and sky will wear out and fade before one word He speaks loses its power or fails to accomplish its purpose. God wants to have that kind of impact through surrendered human vessels.

When I think about the people of old that lived, they all died. God said to them in Zechariah, "Look at all the prophets of old; they came, they are dead, all your fathers of old, they are dead and gone, but My word remains." So if you ignore the purpose for which God gave you life, one day you will evict, you will expire, you will check out of this earth, but the purpose of God stands forever.

So, what is God doing? He's configuring men and women that will give expression to His highest purpose within the time and space given to them. There are some things that today are in huge demand. God is asking you, "Preach," "Win souls," and "Do this." After a while, that's not going to be there anymore. That's how many people lose their fire, their passion, and what God gives to them.

The Psalmist says, "*Thank you for responding to me; you've truly become my salvation! The stone the masons discarded as flawed is now the capstone! This is God's work. We rub our eyes—we can hardly believe it! This is the very day God acted— let's celebrate and be festive! Salvation now, God. Salvation now! Oh yes, God—a free and full life!*" (Psalm 118:21-25 MSG) Don't look at yourself and think, "Well, there's not much that can come out of me." At the age of 80, Moses dreamed God's glory; at the age of 78, Jeremiah began in God's glory. Don't look at what you have or what you don't have. The question is, can God have what you have in terms of your time, your wisdom, your knowledge, your energy?

The widow said to the prophet, "I have nothing but this last food that I will eat. I and my son will die." Yet the prophet said, *"God told me He commanded you to sustain me."* (1 Kings 17:12 ERV) It doesn't make sense! How can God look at, number one, a widow, a woman with no husband? Maybe if the husband was there, the man would say, "Ah, why are you trying to take from my wife? This is our family stuff!" But then a widow—no husband, secondly, a widow, no job, broke, no money. And God said to the prophet, "Go, it's a command."

Yes, what did God see in that widow? God saw a genuine willingness to separate from what she had. If the prophet could tell her and assure her that God had a plan for her life, all she would have was the last meal. And God didn't send the prophet to a millionaire; He sent the prophet to the widow. Somebody has allowed their status to stagnate. So God is saying, "You may not have all of these things, but what I have for you will come from what I have given to you— that little time, that passion, that ability to pray for one hour, that fire for one hour, that soul-winning grace, that little thing."

Even Jesus had to deal with this kind of situation. The Bible tells us, *"But we don't want to upset these people. So go to the lake and throw out a fishing line. Take the first fish you catch and open its mouth. Inside its mouth you will find a four-drachma coin. Take that coin and give it to them. That will pay the temple tax for you and me."* (Matthew 17:27 ERV) And the Bible says many years later, Jesus had to commend and use that woman as an illustration. There's nothing about your life that is not recorded in heaven. So every time you miss a divine opportunity, magnifying excuses, you are given room for evil.

Peter was there; Judas wasn't there. And Jesus said, "We need to pay these taxes." We need to pay; it's not what we should do, but we have to do it. And guess what Peter did? Nothing, because Judas wasn't there. He had the money. So Jesus turned to Peter again and said, "Go and fish." In other words, there are certain times that God feels like you are irresponsible if there is a need, and you won't go out of your way to find a way to supply that need. So every time you say to God, "God, you know if I have, I will give," God said, "Excuse me, have you asked Me? Have you gone to the sea? Have you used what I've given to you?"

The Lord kept saying to me, "There's hope for North America. Things are going to work powerfully." And I kept saying, "Lord, I believe." And the Lord said, "Now it's your people." I said, "God, I don't have anybody; you are the only one I have—your people." No, no, they are your people.

Then the Lord reminded me of the vision I saw of a group of people that looked so admirable, and I saw their leader. With every move he made, things just worked. I was like, "Wow! I need to meet that leader to ask for counsel and to tell me what I'm supposed to do." And when I met him, I found out that I was privileged to be the leader. This, folks, is what happens when we fully surrender to God's purpose. He takes our little and makes it much. He takes our weakness and turns it into strength. He takes our limitations and makes them opportunities for His glory to shine through. The power of surrender isn't about giving up but giving over. It's about allowing God to have His way in every aspect of our lives, trusting that His plans for us are far greater than anything we could imagine for ourselves.

CHAPTER FOUR

CHOSEN FOR GREATNESS

A cts 13:17 (TPT): "The God of Israel chose our forefathers and exalted them during their stay as foreigners in Egypt, and with mighty power, He led them out of that country."

There are people who choose God, but there are people chosen by God. Now, it's amazing when people chosen by God choose God. Do you understand? Now, people who decide to choose God and get accepted in the beloved are powerful, but there are people chosen by God, and when they decide to choose the God that chose them...

Things don't happen by mistake; they don't happen by chance. Manifesting specific dimensions is impossible until there is a divine agreement and arrangement. Our ancestors were divinely chosen to be His people. The God of Heaven divinely chooses you to be His representatives. To be His people—not just where you are now but across the globe.

Most people don't understand that the reason there's a flaw in a certain system is so that they come in and have a place and have a say. Because if you come into a perfect system, you are almost insignificant. The reason there's a flaw in your family is because God wanted you to also have a voice. You were born into a flawed family because God has been counting and was counting and is still counting on you to fix the flaws of your family—not to become an addition to the family flaws, not to come and begin to curse everybody for being bad. "Oh, my life would have been better if my mother was not a drug addict. My life would have been better if my father was not on drugs."

No, The one choice God didn't give you the privilege of making is the father and mother that brought you to this earth. And if you believe that God is the all-wise God, He knew your father was a dopehead, your mother was something out there. Yet He brought you into that family through that family, not just to come in and be a part of the problem, but to come in and not just solve the problem of the family but to be the one God will use to tell the whole world that there's nothing that is so flawed that God cannot turn into wonders.

The Bible says in Psalms 118:22 msg that the stone that the masons ignored has become the chief cornerstone. They said, "This is a flawed stone." He says, "Suddenly this same stone has become the most significant stone that we have."

We will rub our eyes in disbelief. It's not possible! The very stone the masons rejected has turned out to be the most crucial capstone of the act holding up the very house of God. God will get glory out of your life! I said the flaws in your family, God is the answer, but you are the instrument. The house of God will be held up in high esteem through you!

> Psalm 118:23 (NIV): *"The Lord has done this,*
> *and it is marvelous in our eyes."*

There are things your job can do, things your friends can do, your parents can do, and your spiritual parents can do, but there are things only the Living God can do! There are things God can assign angels to do; there are things God can assign prophets to do; there are things God will assign apostles to do, but God takes full responsibility for.

The Lord Himself is the one who has done this, and it's so amazing, so marvelous to see. That's said

God's Divine Selection And Purpose

Acts 13:17 (ERV): *"The God of the people of Israel chose our ancestors and made them great when they were in Egypt. With mighty power, he led them out of that country."*

God didn't merely choose their ancestors to occupy a space in history; He called them to be His possession, His people, His property, His own. This is not a trivial matter because not everyone is divinely chosen, and therein lies the mystery and majesty of God's selection. I recall a Saturday night when God opened my eyes to this scripture while praying. I had encountered this passage countless times, yet that night, it hit me in a way that was entirely new and revitalizing.

When I went to the church where I preach on Sundays, the atmosphere was charged with an explosion of divine energy! Such an anointing enveloped me; it was as if God had ignited a fire within my spirit. I prayed for what felt like an hour and a half without pause, and during that time, every little phrase, every letter, every word entered my spirit, causing my spirit man to be supercharged with His presence. The experience was transformative, and I felt the depth of God's message that He was imparting to me. Not only did He divinely choose our ancestors, but He made them great while they were enslaved in Egypt.

God didn't wait for deliverance to bring greatness. He brought greatness even before deliverance occurred. This aspect of God's character is crucial for us to grasp. It serves as a reminder that even when we find ourselves in the depths of trials, struggles, or enslavement—figuratively speaking—God is already orchestrating greatness in our lives. Our circumstances do not limit him; rather, He transcends them. It's vital to remember that when the greatness God lays upon us manifests, we must remain grounded in our relationship with Him. There is a danger in allowing our newfound greatness to become a distraction, leading us away from the very source of our strength.

The truth is that God has given us grace that unlocks greatness in our lives. We must navigate this with wisdom and discernment. We must guard against the tendency to let what God gives us or what He is creating within us become an idol, becoming more important to us than our relationship with Him. In this sense, the best way to thrive in our walk with God is to understand that our highest form of security lies in personally knowing who God is to us. This relationship supersedes all material possessions or worldly accomplishments.

That's what Jesus meant when He talk with a rich young ruler. The man approached Jesus, stating, "I have done all this from my youth," and his wealth was apparent. Jesus saw the sincerity in his heart but understood that this man had a fundamental barrier to fully embracing the kingdom of God. "One thing you lack," Jesus told him, "Go and sell everything you have, give the money to the poor, come and follow me." The response of the rich young ruler was striking; he left sorrowfully, for he had many riches that were, in fact, possessing him rather than him possessing them.

This is a critical distinction. He didn't leave sorrowful because he lost his riches; he left sorrowful because his riches had him. The crux of the matter is that we can become so materialistic, so consumed with the pursuit of worldly wealth, that we unintentionally become enemies of God. Our God desires for material things to accompany us while goodness and mercy follow closely behind. We should not be chasing after material possessions at the expense of our relationship with God. The rich young ruler's sorrow stemmed from a heart condition; he had allowed his wealth to become his highest sense of security, eclipsing his relationship with the divine.

Some of my pastors asked a question about that verse, I said I know that each of us has areas where God is at work, shaping and molding us. However, the one area that can cause God to look at us with disfavor is when He finds that deep within our hearts, we cling to things that give us a sense of security more than Him. It is in this context that God sometimes strips us of these securities. Yet, there is no need for Him to take away what we hold dear if we willingly offer it up to Him. If we can surrender it all, declaring, "God, I give You everything. If I sing, I sing for You; if I shout, it's for You; if I dance, Lord, there's nothing I have or am that gives me my highest sense of security but You—nothing but You," we open ourselves to a more significant relationship with Him.

Today, the rich young ruler has long since passed into obscurity; we don't even know his name. We refer to him only as the rich young ruler in the other look at Peter, James, and John—the sons of Zebedee—who abandoned their nets, their father, and their livelihood to follow Jesus. Their names are forever etched in the annals of history as faithful servants of the Most High. Every time a preacher preaches today, he will Peter said, no one refer to unless if you want to about him in the negatively.

So when the curtain of history finally gets drawn back, what side will you find yourself on? The answer rests with you, and I am confident that God is working in and around us to ensure He becomes our all in all. That said.

> Acts 13:17 (ERV): *"The God of the people of Israel chose our ancestors and made them great when they were in Egypt. With mighty power, he led them out of that country."*

Amid their slavery, God made His chosen people great. God whispered to my heart, "I don't have to fix everything in their lives to make them great. I will make them great, and through that process, I will address so many of their issues." This is a powerful truth that speaks directly to us today. It tells us we do not have to wait for perfect circumstances to experience greatness. Instead, we are called to rise above our situations and embrace the greatness that God has already placed within us. Certain areas in your life may feel gray or ambiguous; perhaps they seem unworthy of greatness. You must confront those areas with God's authority and flush out any contradictions that may be lingering in your spirit. Stand firm in your faith, and do not allow the doubts or fears of this world to diminish your understanding of who you are in Christ. You are a child of the King! Whatever does not glorify God in your life must disappear as you align yourself with His purpose.

God made His chosen people great, both in numbers and in strength. Your greatness is not an isolated event; it carries the power to draw others to God. True greatness is only recognized when others start to chase it! This is a promise and a calling for each of us. God declares, "I will make your name great; you will be a blessing! You will be blessed until you become a blessing to others." People should start pursuing God's work in your life, and as you chase after Him, those around you will begin to notice the transformation.

Zechariah 8:23 (ERV): *"The Lord All-Powerful says, 'In those days, ten men from all languages and nations will take hold of one Jew by the hem of his robe and say, "Let us go with you because we have heard that God is with you."'*

God's presence in our lives can draw others to Him. In those days, many foreigners would come, speaking different languages, and they would grasp the hem of our robes and say, "We are with you!" Imagine this scenario: your presence commands the attention of ten people who desire to know the God you serve. This is not merely a lofty aspiration but a tangible reality that awaits every believer who dares to embrace their divine selection and purpose.

You must not look at yourself through the lens of doubt or inadequacy. As long as you are a believer, a divine DNA exists within you—a God-given potential that cannot be denied. We are a people chosen by God, and you must cultivate that mentality within your spirit. Picture an average Jewish man; regardless of how dire their circumstances might be, they walk with their heads held high, embodying pride and resilience. Yes, even the poorest among them carry an air of dignity and confidence because they are acutely aware that they are part of something larger than themselves. They are connected to a prophecy that speaks of their identity and the destiny that lies ahead for their children.

The richness of this truth cannot be overstated. Just as God chose Israel, He has chosen you, too. His divine selection comes with a purpose, and it is essential that you live in alignment with that purpose. God does not merely want to bless you; He desires to make you a vessel of blessing for others.

Rejecting Limitations And Embracing Destiny

when Saul forgot who he was, Goliath intimidated him and Israel for 40 days. It took a 17-year-old boy who was just coming to bring food to brethren to remedy the situation. when he got there, the devil made another mistake. Goliath came, and he roared, and that 17-year-old boy said, "Excuse me! What did this idiot say?" He didn't say, "Excuse me, what shall be given because this man is reproaching us?" David described him as: "This uncircumcised Philistine?" That means this guy is not a son of Abraham. He is not part of the covenant. see

David's words show a mindset that refuses to be limited by the size of the challenge. He didn't flinch; he didn't back down in fear. Instead, he stood up boldly, challenging the status quo with a fierce resolve that can only come from a deep understanding of his identity in God. While the whole of Israel cowered in fear at the sight of Goliath, here was a young boy who recognized that the giant was not only a physical threat but also a spiritual insult to the God of Israel. David had clarity about his lineage; he understood the covenant God had made with His people, which set him apart from those with no such claim.

What is essential for us to learn here is that David saw beyond the immediate intimidation posed by Goliath. His declaration, "Who is this uncircumcised Philistine?" wasn't merely a boast; it was a statement of faith. It reflected an awareness that his God was more significant than any giant that stood before him. In our lives, we must cultivate this same mentality—a refusal to bow to the limitations that fear and doubt seek to impose upon us.

Too often, we allow the enormity of our circumstances to define us. When we confront obstacles—be they in our careers, relationships, or personal growth—we may feel like the Israelites, frozen in place by fear. But what David exemplifies is a paradigm shift; he saw his identity in God and realized that this gave him the right to confront the enemy with confidence. It is imperative to understand that you are chosen by God, crafted for greatness, and designed to accomplish what seems impossible.

> 1 Samuel 17:26 (TLB): *"David talked to others standing there to verify the report. 'What will a man get for killing this Philistine and ending his insults unto Israel?' he asked them. 'Who is this heathen Philistine, uncircumcised anyway, that he is allowed?'"*

You see, if you don't understand that God chooses you, you risk living as just another church member, missing out on the depth of what it means to walk in His purpose. When you understand your divine selection, it transforms your perspective. You stop viewing yourself as a mere participant and start recognizing your role as an active player in God's unfolding narrative. You realize that you're not just going through the motions but engaging in a divine drama where you have been given a starring role.

David understood this. He didn't just casually wonder about the rewards for defeating Goliath; he was driven by a righteous indignation that demanded action. He saw that allowing the uncircumcised Philistine to defy the armies of the living God was an insult to his identity and heritage. His passionate response shows that he is aware of his destiny: the conviction that you cannot allow any entity—be it a person, situation, or even your doubts—to challenge the purpose God has placed on your life.

God crafted you; He made you! What flows in your spiritual DNA is beyond your wildest imagination! There's an inheritance that comes from being part of God's family. Just as David had a lineage filled with prophetic promise, so do we inherit a legacy rich with divine purpose.

From the very beginning, the prophecies spoken over our lives are catalysts that propel us toward our destiny. The words of Kenneth Hagin and the prophecies from my father, Dr. David, alongside the mentorship of Dr. George, are not just mere stories; they are signposts in the road of destiny.

David was keenly aware of the covenant that set him apart from his adversary. In the same way, we must recognize that our position in Christ is one of privilege, empowerment, and victory. When you internalize this truth, you become unstoppable. You begin to reject the limitations that the world or your own fears impose upon you, instead embracing the fullness of your destiny with both hands.

The battle against limitations often starts in our minds. Goliath's taunts were not just physical threats; they were psychological warfare aimed at instilling fear and doubt among the Israelites. For 40 days, the Israelites heard Goliath's challenges and each time, it chipped away at their confidence and resolve. It was a battle of perception—a struggle to maintain faith amid overwhelming odds. David, however, came with a different perspective. His boldness in the face of intimidation was rooted in his unwavering faith in God. He refused to let fear dictate his actions; instead, he engaged his mind and heart in a battle of belief. We must learn to do the same.

Many of us face daily challenges that try to pull us down, but just like David, we must train ourselves to look beyond the immediate threat. Our thoughts can either be a launchpad to our destiny or a prison that keeps us locked in mediocrity. Refuse to give power to the voices of doubt and negativity that echo around you. Instead, echo the truths of who God says you are.

Interestingly, David didn't go into battle armed with swords and spears. He went to the stream and picked five stones. He didn't need a full arsenal to achieve victory; all he needed was the right mindset and the confidence to act on it. He picked five smooth stones, knowing that one would be enough for a victory.

From today, every move you make will hit the target! Whether in your career, business ventures, financial decisions, family life, marital choices, or ministry, you will hit the target! But this assurance comes with a responsibility: you must actively engage with your faith and take steps toward your goals. David didn't just sit back and wait for victory to be handed to him; he actively sought it out.

This means being intentional about the decisions you make. In relationships, for example, you cannot allow desperation to dictate your choices. The pressure to settle for less can be overwhelming, especially when you see your peers making choices that you feel you should also make. But remember, your destiny is not determined by others; it is uniquely yours to embrace.

Be wary of distractions that seek to undermine your progress. In the pursuit of greatness, some individuals may unintentionally become obstacles rather than allies. David's brothers questioned his motives, not understanding the fire that burned within him. In the same way, those close to us may not always understand the paths we are called to walk. Some may advise you to take the easier route or to settle for mediocrity, simply because they have not grasped the greatness God has placed within you. Don't allow their doubts to seep into your spirit. Remember that your calling is distinct and comes with divine purpose.

CHAPTER FIVE

ORCHESTRATING YOUR STANDING OUT

We know that it is God's will for us to stand out. Everyone who walked with God testified who they were different from others. God never treats His faithful followers the way He treats every human being. Don't ever let people make you think that we are all equal in the eyes of God. We are not equal in the eyes of God! God doesn't treat us equally.

However, there is an equalizer in the spirit realm that whoever understands the secrets of God will be able to walk with God to orchestrate their preferential treatment. God is such a glorious God that He likes it when anything He signs on stands out. Don't think that the moment God signs on a thing, it must stand out. It's not so. The signature of God is supposed to be like the sun in the sky, a star in the sky. The moment God signs on your head, it's impossible for you not to be ahead. However, many people had God's signature on their head and messed it up.

It's possible to mess up God's signature. Paul said, *"I'm crucified with Christ; nevertheless, I live; yet not I, but Christ that lives in me. The life I now live in the flesh I live by the faith of the Son of God who loved me and gave Himself for me."* Galatians 2:20 (KJV).

He said, who loves me so much that He gave Himself for me and dispensed His life into me. That's what salvation is: God dispensing the life of Christ into man. But there are many believers, unfortunately, that after God dispenses Himself into them, they dispense God to nowhere!

He said, "And dispenses His life into mine." Look at verse 21 (TPT). *"So that is why I don't view God's grace as something minor or peripheral." I don't view God's grace as something minor! Most of us not don't understand the fullness of the benefits of what God has given to us. Some have a sense of it, but their view of it has limited the grace of God! He said, "The problem with many people is how they view grace. God gives me a car and decides to give you grace!"*

The grace God gives you has the car, has the fuel, has insurance. No, that's not enough; it has protection for the future car! Because the grace of God is superabundant, and it multiplies with faithful use.

It multiplies with faithful use! You pray, God give me a car, and then one car comes, and you're happy! And so, you start begging God repeatedly, "Where's your car? I couldn't drive!" "What happened?" "No gas!" "No money for gas!" "Where's your car?" "I couldn't drive; it has engine problems!" Whereas the grace of God is the grease that makes your life run smoothly!

Unfortunately, many believers have commonized the grace! If you ask God for a house and God decides to give you grace, it's because everything to ensure that house and happiness, fulfillment, and success in that house is in grace! Grace is not minor! Grace is not for rent; it's not like your effort. The effort is great, but grace is different!

The King James says, "I do not frustrate the grace of God." So when God decides to dispense His life in you, everything that will make your life count is in that life of Christ! Why is it that many don't express the fullness of God? They frustrate the grace!

> Genesis 2:1-3. KJV *Thus the heavens and the earth were finished, and all the host of them. And on the seventh day, God ended His work which He had made, and He rested on the seventh day from all His work which He had made. And*

God blessed the seventh day and sanctified it because He had rested from all His work which God created and made.

Verse 3-5 TLB: And God blessed the seventh day and declared it holy because it was the day when He ceased this work of creation. Here is a summary of the events in the creation of heaven and earth when the Lord God made them. No plants or grain were sprouting up across the earth at first.

What was lacking from the earth or on the earth? There were no plants or grain sprouting up. This was before there were plants on the earth. Nothing was growing in the fields because the Lord God had not made it rain on the earth!

Why didn't God send rain? There was no one to care for it! God didn't send rain. There were no plants because there was no rain! There was no rain because there was no man! No one to care for what God permits to grow!

Don't tell me that you're a failure because God has no plan for your life! Your biggest battle is in your inability to recognize that God is waiting for you to wake up to the equation, to the occasion! Because rain is waiting for man!

God is in search; He's looking for a man, a woman, a boy, a girl —someone who understands how God wants things done and someone who will accept responsibility for caring for success!

If God said there was no man to care for the plants, on that note, I will not send rain! What do you think God is saying when He finds a man or woman who says, "God, I'm going to care for what You care for! I'm going to care for what You are interested in! Lord, I may not have much or no more, but one thing I will not do is to sit down and watch life without things growing!"

God never opened His mouth to call Deborah, "My daughter, Deborah, from today you are the prophetess of Israel! From today, you are the woman of God! If thou openest thy mouth to prophesy, I will give thee Thy word."

Judges 5:6-7 (TPT) *"During the days of Shamgar, son of Anath, and the days of Jael, the highways were abandoned, and travelers walked the winding paths. The villagers in Israel would not fight; they held back until I, Deborah, arose—until I arose to be a mother for Israel."*

There are highways in the spirit, but there are highways on earth, and God said, "My ways are higher than your ways." God will connect you to His highways, and you will become the one that will allow travelers to use the highways. Because of you, people will serve God better in the name of Jesus!

Country towns were no more in Israel until you, Deborah, came up! Until you came up as a mother. You say, oh, I wish we had evangelists in the church, and God is saying, "Oh, I wish you rise as an evangelist!" Oh, I wish we had billionaires in the kingdom, and God is saying, ""Oh, I wish you accept the call to being a multi-billionaire!" Not that you are claiming billionaire, but you'll be sleeping eight hours. No billionaire sleeps eight hours —that's laziness. Lazy people end up having nothing. You'll be a billionaire, but there are no prophets. God says, "I'm calling you to be the prophet!"

Your only problem is that you are a noise maker; you talk too much. Prophets don't talk too much. When God calls you aside, He wants to talk to you, but you're too distracted. You find it difficult to coordinate yourself, to be still and know that He is God. Your soul is too distracted for God to show you things. Even if God shows you, He shows you just 1% of what you need to see, and then you see one thing and conclude, "I have seen it all!"

No! When God shows you one thing, there are a hundred other things attached to that one thing. That's why the sun you see has many rays. The rainbow has many rays—over fifty-something billion colors from that tiny seven-color rainbow. The more you look, the more you see, but many people are too distracted in their souls. They are so distracted that when they want to go to bed, their spirit is so scattered everywhere that by the time they sleep, only monkeys and gorillas show up in their dreams! Even when angels want to come, the monkeys in their dreams chase them away.

God turns ashes into beauty; some people see only ashes instead of beauty. Until I, Deborah arose as a mother in Israel. Amplified says, "Until you came up." So, the abandonment was a result of what? There is a lack of individuals who will orchestrate their stand because they are waiting to stand together with everybody else.

......Villages were unoccupied, and rulers ceased

Not in my days. God didn't send rain because plants would become weeds and wilderness if they grew. That means the moment God finds personal interest in caring for what He cares for, God will suddenly cause things to grow. Someone—your finances haven't grown because God knows that if it grows, you will care for yourself but never for Him. Unbelievers can do that, not you. Because we are stewards, God is watching to see how much you can handle. Do you know that in all of man's creation, the only thing God put side by side with Himself that seeks worship is money?

Mammon! If I sweat to labor, and I labor, and I bring in money, and God says to me, "I need every single thing," guess what? I can say, "God, it's my sweat!" Or I can say, "God, I give You my sweat, give me Your sweet!"

> Matthew 6:24 ERV. *"It's not possible to serve two masters.*
> *You'll be loyal to one and not care about the other. You*
> *cannot serve God and money at the same time."*

"Oh, I'm not serving money." No, but money controls you. If you never come to a place where you understand that everything, down to the last penny you have, belongs to God, God will let you use your sweat and your energy to get things. God is not stupid! God knows that you need to be cared for. And yet God watches because He wants to bring you to a place where what looks like your yearly care becomes less than your daily care. What you put aside as a budget for your yearly care, including your rent, your mortgage, your phone bills, your hair, your health, your eyelashes, your medical bills, your clothes—everything you put aside as a yearly budget to care for yourself— God will answer them in one encounter.

Man God's Steward

Genesis 2 10. KJV A river flowed from Eden. It watered the garden. The river then separated and became four small rivers.

Who gave the river intelligence to separate?

The river flowed and watered the garden. If you go further, verses 8 and 9 say God planted a garden eastward of Eden. Follow this story, right? God said, "I'm done with creation," and before God rested, He decided to plant a garden. After planting the garden, He allowed a river to flow.

A garden is a small portion of a landscape called Earth. God decided to take a little portion of that landscape and work out a specific thing. That landscape's features automatically differed from everything else on the earth. Lord, the dry ground outside was so rough and difficult that if you lived outside of Eden, you would think it was a useless place to live. Yet eastward, 4836 West 13th Street, was a garden.

After working for six days, He didn't finish His work until He planted a garden—a space where the reality of heaven was present. The ugliness of hell was outside that space. The garden was so pretty, so powerful, so loaded that it was not affected by the dryness that was outside the garden.

The Lord God planted a garden in the east, in a place named Eden. Eden in the original Hebrew means "Presence." My presence, My presence. So what did He do?

Verse 8: *"And the Lord God planted a garden eastward in Eden; and there he put the man whom he had formed."*

Salvation is your automatic ticket to that garden! When you received Christ, you were put in that garden. Because Eden means "Presence," and Christ brings you the presence of God. So you are in that garden!

Verse 9; *"And out of the ground made the Lord God to grow every tree that is pleasant to the sight, and good for food; the tree of life also in the midst of the garden, and the tree of the knowledge of good and evil."*

Every good thing begins to grow. Let me take you back a bit to verses 3 and 4

"These are the generations of the heavens and of the earth when they were created, in the day that the Lord God made the earth and the heavens, And every plant of the field before it was in the earth, and every herb of the field before it grew: for the Lord God had not caused it to rain upon the earth, and there was not a man to till the ground."

Nothing grew because there was no one to care for whatever grew. I'm asking you, what statement is the absence of beautiful things in your life making? What statement is the absence of beautiful things in your life making?

You scream you sing, you shout, you dance, but your beauty is becoming ashes instead of ashes becoming beauty! So, the lack of beauty in a person's life, the presence of constant depression, unhappiness, fear, cowardice, confusion, "I don't even know what to do," "Nothing is working in my life"—all of these things, they are making a statement. They are telling you that God doesn't trust your ability to care for good things He's about to grow in your life.

You can say, "No, it's not true," but you see the patterns? That's the pattern of God. "God, if You give me a man of God, I will serve You forever!" God knows by the time you have that man of God, within one month, you'll slap him 17 times.

God knows that the generation He's raising is a generation of men and women that will be so sold out to Him. Don't get me wrong, God will always have careless, callous people. You might even be one of those, so God will not break His head over you—He won't! But in the midst of careless, callous, irresponsible people, God will always have men and women.

Acts 13:22 (MSG) *"But God removed Saul and put King David in his place, with this commendation: 'I've searched the land and found this David, son of Jesse. He's a man whose heart beats to my heart, a man who will do what I tell him to do.'"*

The moment God finds you, promotion follows. Once God finds you, you are automatically a ruler. Why did God back Deborah up? She had that commendation that in her lifetime villages would be occupied, vagabonds would leave the street. All those soldiers who are not soldiers would leave the street or wake up again in the same land. There was a man called Barak. Barak was supposed to be a powerful man, but he had a chicken heart. Can you imagine? God had to raise a woman to awaken the soldier in Barak.

Your place is waiting for your commendation. God is saying, "I will not do it in spite of you; I will do it because of you." You have to align. Align or fall out. And God is not waiting for your perfection; God is waiting for your consecration—your personal decision to orchestrate your standing out. You have to trust me, prophetic things can be crazy.

"......Public roads were abandoned. Travelers went by back roads"

Not in your lifetime. These days, Christians will be bold because of you. Believers will be bold because of you. Stephen brought boldness to the faith. Philip brought boldness to the faith. David and Philemon brought, and are bringing, boldness to Christianity. You will bring boldness to the body of Christ in the name of Jesus.

Warriors became fat and sloppy; no fight left in them. What a disease. Yes, sir. That's why when something little offends them, they won't go to church. How can you be serving God and someone says something that offends you, and you stop going to church? Is it God that said that? You see bastards everywhere claiming they're called, familiar spirits taking people out of the body of Christ. The spirit of can only destroy them. Lovers of themselves, don't tell me that you can serve God effectively on your own if you have not faithfully served God in another man's vineyard. Even God allowed Moses to prove his faithfulness for 40 years, sir, taking care of the flock of his father-in-law.

> Judges 5:6-8 (MSG) *In the days of Shamgar son of Anath, in the days of Jael, the main roads were abandoned; travelers went by back roads. The village life in Israel was shattered; it was shattered until I, Deborah, arose, a mother in Israel. When they chose new gods, war came to the city gates. Not a shield or spear could be seen among forty thousand in Israel."*

No fight left in warriors; that's a problem. Satan is constantly looking for ways to take your fight out of you. Depression: every little thing makes you depressed. They say your nose is big; you check the mirror 17 times, forgetting that if your nose is big, it's because God spent extra time giving you a big nose. They say your nose is small; you're wondering how to make it big, not knowing that God wanted your nose to be the size to fit your assignment. There's no mistake with God. You will make it.

These people are soldiers, warriors; they became sloppy, and her husband was a prophet. Thank God for the husband. We should respect him because there are some men that are so insecure about the calling of their women. Yet, there are some women that will kill their husbands for pursuing the call of God on their lives. And yet there are some women that will give up anything and everything just to be with a man that knows that this is what God has called him to do. The same thing with men. There are some men who will give up anything just to be with a woman that says, "You and I, we do the work of God together."

And the work of God doesn't mean we stand on the pulpit and preach. It can be a politician; it can be an entrepreneur, a businessman; it can be a teacher; it can be just anything. So long as you have decided to arise and awaken the warrior within you.

Warriors became fat and sloppy, yet her husband was a prophet. No fight left in them; only flight. When lions and bears come, they run away. And when they run away, they go and testify, "A lion and a bear came against me, and glory to God, I escaped!" And another little boy says, "Are you people running away from lions and bears?

Another is running to lions and bears! Who do you think God will pick?" If you were God, who would you pick? You would not run away.

Awakening Your Spiritual Potential

When there was no one to care for it God said, "I'm not going to let anything grow." So I'm still asking you the question: what statement is the lack of beauty in your life making? Thank God for your clothes, your hair, your eyelashes, your nice hairstyle, but that's not the description of beauty, because all of these things fade away. Thank God for your makeup. When you wash it off, you see what you really look like. And I know you're beautiful. Come on, man, I'm not laughing; you're beautiful. You're beautiful.

Yeah, but the reality is that it fits. No matter how clean you brush your teeth before you go to bed—sleep 4 hours, 2 hours, 3 hours—when you wake up, you know what your mouth smells like. You understand? So, none of these things are good, but that's not the beauty we're talking about. The real beauty of Christianity is because you said, "Oh, Hallelujah" in the morning. Demons are screaming and looking for where to hide.

That's it! No. You just woke up in the morning; you have not even started praying, and all the demons start telling themselves, "He's up! She's up!" And they start taking cover, looking for where to hide. Beauty is when demons tremble at your presence. Beauty is not when you use your physical looks to seduce everybody in the church. That is demonic; that's evil.

You are taking away strength from people. You are becoming an agent of Satan. That's evil; that's not beauty. It's going to fade, and God will make sure it fades very fast. Instead of casting out demons, you are bringing demons into people's lives. You are delivered; I say you are delivered.

So watch it. That's what Satan is doing now. His fresh mission is recycling agents of demons into churches—agents of Satan. His agents. He sends them from church to church. By the time they go to this church and have destroyed everybody, they say, "I don't like the church." They move to the next church. And when they go to a church and find out that the people taking care of that garden cannot be destroyed, they find a story and get angry, and they leave. They go to where they can walk in this house.

Fire! God can bring deliverance. Just don't make yourself an agent of darkness. Beauty is not when you manipulate people and have your way. That's not beauty; that's evil. That's wickedness, and you will be judged. God will judge you for that. You will be judged.

Beauty is when, because of you, people are eager to embrace the call of God. Barak would not go out and do anything for the Lord, yet he was a warrior. So Deborah called him. She said, "Call me Barak." And when Barak came, God began to talk to him and gave him the word of the Lord. He said, "How can you be a warrior, and under your nose, there's no beauty in Israel? Villages and houses are abandoned." And she started talking to him. She said, "Thus says the Lord, I'm going to defeat Jabin. I will defeat Sisera. I will hand him over to you. Go and fight! Don't sit down here and use your muscles to intimidate people. Don't sit down here and use your beauty to intimidate people."

> Judges 5:12 (ERV): *"Wake up! Wake up, Deborah!*
> *Wake up! Wake up and sing a song! Get up, Barak!*
> *Capture your captives, son of Abinoam!"*

Barak means blessing, but the blessing had become dormant because he was not using it to be an overflow to expand in the kingdom of God. And the woman said, "Get up! Get up out of that grave! Get up!"

Barak, wake up! Deborah was what she told herself. She said, "Honey, can't you do something about it?" And the husband said, "Babe, what are you talking about? It's too difficult. How can we go to—I mean, sorry. What are you talking about? It's too difficult. How can we go to places where we can be arrested, kidnapped, or stuff? How can we do this?" And the man kept talking to her, and she said, "Okay, I love you, honey, I love you." But then, when she gets back and closes her eyes, she says, "Wake up, Deborah! Wake up!"

Somebody tell yourself, "Wake up! Call your name! Say, 'Wake up!'" If nobody wakes you up, wake yourself up. If God doesn't call you, call yourself to God. God is still in the business of searching the land, looking for men, looking for women, looking for boys, looking for girls. God will lift you up. I said God will lift you up. When I hear your amen, receive your wake-up call.

You can orchestrate your standing out. There are times God Himself will be the one to cause you to stand out. But there are certain things God has released in the atmosphere, and God is saying you can follow certain principles, and as you follow them, you orchestrate your stand-out.

Nobody knew Deborah except that we know her husband was a prophet. But suddenly, she woke herself up. Sometimes, one wake-up call will not be enough. Wake yourself up! Call your name! Tell yourself, "What's going on? Why are you sleeping? Where's your prayer fire? Where's your anointing? Where's your beauty? Where's your beauty? Where are your songs?"

Beauty is when your talent is now blessing humanity. Beauty is when demons tremble at your presence. Beauty is when you have the ability to connect with the spirit world and look at ashes and turn ashes into beauty. Say to your neighbor, "I'm beautiful! I'm beautiful! I don't know about you, but I'm beautiful!" Don't look at my outward appearance; it has very little to do with my true beauty. Wait and see! Now that I am waking up, I am awakened as a lion that was sleeping. I awake. Wake up!

Your waking up is considered a true awakening when your spirituality awakens others. Barak is not necessarily a male; Barak is a spirit—the spirit of a warrior. Suddenly, you have been touched by God, and destiny causes you to wake up. What many cannot do to themselves, you decide to do. God, I am making myself that man who will care for the ground and let beautiful things grow. Let beautiful things grow.

CHAPTER SIX

CATEGORIES OF PEOPLE IN THE CHURCH

People Who By Their Waking Up Put Others To Sleep

In the church, we encounter all manner of people. There are those who, by their very awakening, seem to have a knack for put others into spiritual slumber. These people aren't your run-of-the-mill churchgoers; they're a special breed, characterized by a potent brew of insecurity, bitterness, and jealousy that'd make even the devil blush. They're the ones that can't stand to see anyone else shine because, in their twisted minds, someone else's light might just cast a shadow on their own lambent candle.

These people are not always aware of what they're doing. Some of them might even think they're doing the Lord's work, keeping things in check, maintaining the status quo. But let me tell you, the moment someone starts rising up or catching the spotlight, these spiritual sleep-inducers kick into high gear. It's like they've got a sixth sense for detecting potential threats to their perceived position or influence.

What we're dealing with here is not just petty church politics or harmless competition. Nah, this is straight-up witchcraft in the house of God. And I am not talking about no hocus-pocus, magic wand type of witchcraft. I'm talking about the kind of spiritual manipulation that can suck the life right out of a thriving ministry or a blossoming believer. You can see that in the life of Saul.

Saul had been coasting along, doing his kingly thing, not really taking his God-given responsibilities all that seriously. But the moment he caught wind of this young upstart named David, suddenly Saul was wide awake and ready to run a marathon. But instead of using that awakening to mentor the young one, to pour into him and say, "Listen here, David, I've made some royal mistake in my time. Let me show you the ropes so you don't repeat my mistakes. You're going be the next big thing in Israel, and I want to make sure you're ready for it. My boy Jonathan? He's going be your right-hand man. Together, we're going to make Israel shine brighter than a diamond in the desert sun" - instead of all that, what does Saul do? He spends years - years, I tell you - chasing this poor kid all over the place, trying to put him in an early grave.

We don't see that kind of thing nowadays." But let me tell you, brothers and sisters, this same spirit is alive and kicking in our churches today. It's in the pastor who can't stand to see his associate minister gaining popularity. It's in the long-time church member who uses their influence to shut down every new idea from the young folks. It's in the worship leader who subtly sabotages the talented newcomer because they're afraid of losing their spot-on stage. This isn't just about hurt feelings or bruised egos. When these sleep-inducers get to work, they rob the entire body of Christ of the gifts and callings God distributed among His people. They create an environment where toeing the line is more important than walking in the Spirit, where keeping things the way they've always been takes precedence over letting the Holy Ghost move in fresh, new ways.

This behavior sets a dangerous precedent in the church. It teaches the younger generation that success in ministry is about playing politics and jockeying for position rather than serving God with a pure heart and submitting to His will. It perpetuates a cycle of fear and control that's as far from the freedom Christ promised us as the East is from the West. The real tragedy here is that these people who wake up to put others to sleep often don't even realize the damage they're doing. They're so caught up in their own insecurities, so focused on protecting their little piece of the pie, that they can't see how they're stunting the growth of the entire body. They become unwitting agents of the enemy, sowing discord and division where there should be unity and mutual edification.

People Who By Their Waking Up, Weakened Believers In Church

These people have a special kind of problem because, on the surface, it might look like they're growing like they're really getting into this whole Christianity thing. But underneath, they're bringing a world of hurt into the church, and they're dragging others down with them. The issue with these people is that they never let God deliver them 1 John 2:16 (KJV): *From the "For all that is in the world, the lust of the flesh, and the lust of the eyes, and the pride of life, is not of the Father, but is of the world."* They're rising up in the church, sure, but they're using what God's given them to strengthen the body of Christ to weaken other folks instead. It's like they've got one foot in the Kingdom and one foot firmly planted in the world, and they're doing the splits between the two.

God will let you come as you are. He is not expecting you to have it all together before you darken the door of a church. But here's the kicker - He hates it when you stay as you came in. You can come as you are, but for the love of all that's holy, don't stay as you came! There will be a change, and I'm talking about a radical, turn-your-world-upside-down kind of change. You have to crucify that flesh and put it to death daily because if you don't, it's going to wreak havoc in the body of Christ.

You've got believers bringing their worldly gossip life into the church, turning prayer requests into a spiritual TMZ. You've got others bringing their greed, trying to turn the house of God into some kind of holy casino. And don't even get me started on the ones who bring their crookedness, thinking they can pull the wool over God's eyes just because they fooled the church folks. But the worst of the bunch? The ones that get under my skin? It's the believers who bring their promiscuous life into the body of Christ. In the world, they were sleeping with ten men and 20 women, living it up like there's no tomorrow. And now they're in Christ, but instead of letting God clean them up, they've multiplied the thing. They're out here distributing evil spirits to different people, even the ones who are trying to strengthen themselves in the Lord.

You've got a brother or a sister who's genuinely trying to walk in holiness. They're doing their best to keep their mind pure, their body a temple of the Holy Spirit. And then along comes one of these so-called "awakened" believers, bringing all their sexual baggage with them. Before you know it, they've found a weak sister or brother, and bam! They've transferred that spirit of lust, that spirit of promiscuity. And it doesn't stop there - it spreads like wildfire, from one person to another, to another, and another.

And let me tell you, it isn't just about the physical act. You've got believers addicted to pornography, filling their minds with all sorts of filth, and then they come and interact with the body of Christ like everything's hunky-dory. Or you've got the ones who are bisexual, swinging both ways, thinking they can have their cake and eat it, too. And the worst part? You don't even know who these people are half the time. They're sitting next to you in the pew, singing the same hymns, quoting the same scriptures, but all the while, they're carrying these evil spirits, these ungodly soul ties, and they're spreading them around like it's communion.

This is serious business, folks. When you open yourself up to these people, let your guard down, and get all cozy with them, you invite evil spirits into your life. And let me tell you, even if God wants to bring beauty to your life, Satan's always going to be there, waiting to contaminate that beauty. That's why you must love your destiny enough not to trade it for a moment of pleasure, a juicy gossip, or a get-rich-quick scheme.

"But we're supposed to love everybody, right? Isn't the church a hospital for sinners, not a museum for saints?" And you're right, to a point. But loving people doesn't mean letting them destroy the church from the inside out. It doesn't mean standing by while they weaken the faith of new believers and lead the vulnerable astray.

The real problem is that these folks have never really understood what it means to be transformed by the renewing of their minds. They've heard the gospel, they've said the sinner's prayer, and they might even be baptized, but they've never let that truth sink down deep into their souls. They're still operating with a worldly mindset, bringing all their old habits, all their old ways of thinking, right into the heart of the church.

And let me tell you, it's a dangerous game they're playing. because while they might think they're getting away with it, while they might fool the people around them for a while, they can't fool God. And the damage they're doing? It's real, and it's lasting. They're not just hurting themselves - they're hurting the entire body of Christ. Think about it - when a new believer sees someone who's been in the church for years still living like the devil, what message does that send? When someone who's struggling with temptation sees a "mature" Christian giving in to every fleshly desire, how does that affect their own fight against sin? It weakens their resolve; it makes them question whether this whole Christianity thing is even real or worth it.

And that's exactly what the enemy wants. He's using these weakened, compromising believers as his trojan horses, sneaking them into the church to destroy it from the inside out. They might look like sheep, they might talk like sheep, but underneath, they're wolves in sheep's clothing, tearing apart the flock one soul at a time.

Attitudes That Make People Become Weakened

People become weakened through your gossip, through your lies. That second category, God dislikes! God dislikes it! People who sow disunity among brethren—God dislikes it! The body of Christ becomes weak when we are disunited, when we are divided. And that's why if a person comes to you and is gossiping and you know that's their habit, for you to keep encouraging them—say, "Well, it's okay, we're going to pray now"—if they say it once, it's different. But if it's becoming their habit, they will say this, they say that, or you see a character that is inconsistent with Christianity, with Christ—you are not obligated to befriend any of them.

You can, as a matter of fact, rebuke them. Say, "No, sister, brother, I don't do this; I don't like this. I don't like it, period." If you entertain it, you will think you are strong. It's impossible! The person down can easily pull the person up than the person up pulling the person down. Disunity weakens the body; it takes away victory and fight from people.

But this is the one that is so crazy. People become weak when you wake up because many people can be nice until they wake up. Until they discover that they're important, God likes it when your importance translates into kingdom expansion. But when your importance now translates into the slumbering and sleeping of believers, or your importance translates into the weakening of other believers that are trying to be strong, then you are giving God no choice but to keep you in a resettlement camp. And if you never allow Him to bring complete deliverance to you, then you may be great in slavery, but greatness is better in freedom. Do you understand?

You may be great in slavery, but greatness is better in freedom. So don't accept the greatness that keeps you a slave. Let there be greatness that makes you sleep with your eyes closed. And when you wake up, you wake up with your eyes open.

Another thing that makes people weak—besides gossip, besides sexual promiscuity, perversion, a dirty mind, dirty heart, disunity

—is a doctrine of compromise. In Revelations 2:14 (TPT), Jesus said, "I hate the doctrine of Balaam," and there was the doctrine of the Nicolaitans. What makes people weak? As a matter of fact, the Bible says there was a woman called a prophetess in the Bible. Revelations says, "But this prophetess seduces all my prophets." So you know that that's not a prophetess of God; that's an agent of Satan.

They do evil without remorse, without repentance, without, "Oh God, please deliver me." But then the doctrine of Balaam and the Nicolaitans is a doctrine of lukewarmness—indifference. Some people, when they awake, their biggest poison to the body of Christ is that in their importance, they sell lukewarmness to people. They commonize holy things. They are the ones that can stand and preach. If you give them a microphone to preach, they can preach for two hours. And you give them 10 minutes, they will say, "Ah, when I—the Spirit took me!" But now, when you, that is supposed to be the one the Spirit takes for two hours, you are doing it, they begin to look at their friends in church.

The moment you say, "Give me five more minutes," they look at each other. They think that it's just a common thing, not knowing that in the presence of God, everything counts. Everything! Even the Bible says there is a curse in the book of Proverbs 10:10 KJV/ TPT - : *it said to those that wink the eye, the winking of the eye is a terrible thing.* To wink the eye—that is, in different contexts, it has a different meaning.

> *He that winketh with the eye causeth sorrow, but the acting fool shall fall. He that winketh with the eye causes trouble; he makes clever plans and won't look you in the eye. But the one who speaks correction honestly can be trusted to make peace.*

Now, these ones, they won't look at you, but they look at their partners. I'm trying to teach you what you must reject from your fellow friends because they are not interested in what you're interested in. They can now, when they awake—that's why such people, their awakening is seasonal. One week, two weeks, they awake, hey! They can be so awake, hype! The next five weeks, you are begging them to look for 1% of the previous awake. It's not there; it's not there. The moment they feel tired in church, they give in to their tiredness. The moment they feel sleepy, they start sleeping. And some, in order not to be embarrassed by sleep, they will leave service in the midst of it.

So you have to watch that your awakeness doesn't weaken others. You may not agree with me, but I believe that one of the reasons God allowed my late sister to go home is because God spoke to me to tell her she was already big. She had become a system; people admired her. God knows everyone. And then the poor women, widows that look up to her admired her. So guess what she started doing? She would take the tithe that you're supposed to give in church to use it to take care of widows. God allowed that until she started telling the widows that you see, sometimes this tithe that I'm supposed to give to church, maybe her tithe is like 2 million naira or something—she said, "I'll use it to empower you people, and I think that God likes it that way." Are you kidding me? That's the spirit of King Soul.

When you become awakened, God is counting on your wakefulness. People admire people. Lady Gaga awoke; she used meat to sew clothes. One of her fans used some grass or something to sew clothes. Because once you are awakened, your life becomes another presence pattern. That's why there are certain things you must never take for granted or do. You don't look and allow weakness to rule you because someone is watching you who is capable of becoming like you.

The Lord gave me a word, and I called—I told my sister, the Lord said I should tell you, this is the dream I saw. She said, "Oh, you are so right." She said, "But I feel like I need to send the tithe to you because all these pastors in Nigeria, you can't trust them." I said, "What if people around me also say they can't trust me?" You know what she said? She said, "Even the devil comes around you; he knows he can trust you."

I said, "No, it's because you know me." She said, "It doesn't take long for people to know you." She said, "I want to send my tithe directly to you." But I said to her, "No, don't send the tithe to me; put it in the church."

She decided to use it. I said, "My Dear, you are not the one that sets the rules. You trust me because you know me." There are people that when they see me, the first thing they do is suspect me. Oh yeah, they'll suspect me!

People have suspected certain things. If you know what people suspected! But one thing is that you don't have to stay long with me. One week, you will know that this person—in fact, one day you will know—I'm a straight shooter. Very simple; straight shooter. So now, it's not everybody that is able to let you see that they are straight shooters.

So I told her, "Don't worry about what the pastors do with the tithe; worry about God; give it." I called her again, and I told her over and over again the reason why God told Moses, "Never ever pray about entering the promised land to me. Don't speak to me of that matter." Why? Because Moses had become a pattern. God said, "Speak to the rock." Moses decided not to speak to the rock; rather, he struck the rock twice. And when he did that, God said, "You can't enter." Why? If Moses had entered the promised land, it would have been difficult for salvation to be perfected by one crucifixion. Jesus had to die and come back alive, and die again that's when salvation would be completed because Moses had become a spiritual pattern.

You have no idea who you are becoming when you stay close to God. You think you are nobody? No, you are already a pattern in the spirit world. You that think you are weak and small but Satan is afraid of you.

People Who By Their Waking Up, Wake Others Up

Proverb 10:10 says, *"If you wink with the eye craftily and with malice causes sorrow, and that sorrow"* is not just for people; it's for the winker. You have to understand, that when you step into the house of God, you are not just walking into any old building. You're stepping into a spiritual portal, with millions of angels on high alert because of you. Not because of the church building, not because of the pastor, but because of you. The security system in heaven is going off like crazy, flashing red, because of how important you are.

God used to send maybe 100 or 1000 angels with some of us. But now? He's multiplying that, sending millions of angels per person. That's how crucial you are in this spiritual battle we're fighting. You might not see it with your physical eyes, but in the spirit realm, it's like Fort Knox up in here!

While at the mission trip. I was preaching in my village, Lantan, and something wild happened. As I was coming down from the pulpit, people were trying to greet me, and the ushers were doing their job, keeping them back. But this one man, dressed in white, stretched out his hand. When I shook it, I knew instantly - this man had come with charm, trying to paralyze himself.

Now, I could've just kept walking, but the Lord said, "Finish it." So I turned back and confronted him. I said, "Really? You came here? I promise you, you'll be a dead man!" He tried to play it off, saying he just wanted me to lay hands on him. But I wasn't born yesterday. I told him, "When has laying hands on you been shaking hands with me? I'm coming back for you." I went back to my seat, then climbed up to preach again. When I came, I told them. I told Reverend Isaiah, "Look at this guy. I told the rest, 'Look at this guy! Keep an eye on him. I said he came with charm to shake David Philemon. I mounted; by the time I was talking, I said, 'Say you are here! You came with charm to shake? You are dead!' By the time I started doing that, six or seven minutes later, the man that was standing by the altar disappeared. He left. That kind of man, you will never live to tell a story again! Never!

That's the kind of power we're dealing with when we truly wake up in the spirit. It's like what happened with Deborah in the Bible. She said, "I awoke. I arose as a mother in Israel." And when she woke up, she didn't keep it to herself. Nah, she woke up Barak too. That's how you know your spiritual awakening is legit, that it's divinely approved. It's when others around you start catching that fire, when they start wanting to do big things for God too. Your inspiration, your revelation, it starts stirring up the destiny in other folks.

Take Barak, for instance. He knew he had become a coward, but when Deborah told him to go fight Sisera, it lit a fire under him. Sure, he was scared at first. "Who are you talking about, Mama? The man with 900 chariots?" But Deborah didn't back down. She said, "Go, because God said I will defeat him for you."

That's the kind of awakening we're talking about. It's not just about you getting your act together. It's about you waking up in such a way that it shakes others out of their spiritual slumber. God is waiting for you to arise so that beauty can come back to the body of Christ. It's like what we see in Genesis 2:8-9. God had created everything, but He was waiting. Waiting for what, you ask? For man to show up and take care of things. It says, "Then the Lord God caused all." When there was a man, then there was growth. When there was a man, then there was beauty. When there was a man, God caused things to grow.

You see, your spiritual awakening is not just about you. It's about you becoming that man, that woman, who God can use to bring growth and beauty to everything around you. When you wake up, really wake up, you become a catalyst for God's power to flow. This are not small thing we're talking about here. It's about you stepping into your divine purpose with such force that it creates a ripple effect in the spirit realm. When you wake up like that, demons tremble, angels rejoice, and other believers start to feel that fire in their bones again.

It's like you become a spiritual alarm clock, jolting others out of their complacency. Suddenly, the lukewarm start getting hot for God again. The ones who've been sitting on the sidelines start suiting up for battle. The ones who've been content with just showing up on Sundays start hungering for more of God's presence. That's the kind of awakening we need in the body of Christ today. Not just individuals getting their lives right, but people waking up in such a way that it causes a chain reaction of spiritual revival. It's about creating an atmosphere where the Holy Spirit can move freely, where miracles become commonplace, where the power of God is on full display.

So I'm asking you - are you ready to wake up like that? Are you ready to be a Deborah, who not only wakes up herself but also stirs up the Baraks around her? Are you ready to be that man, that woman, whose presence causes God to release growth and beauty in the church?

Because let me tell you, when you wake up like that, you become dangerous to the enemy. You become a threat to the status quo. You become a force to be reckoned with in the spiritual realm. And that's exactly what God is looking for - people who are so awake, so on fire for Him, that they can't help but wake others up too.

CHAPTER SEVEN

KEYS FOR YOUR LIFTING

Isaiah 61:3 (KJV): "To appoint unto them that mourn in Zion, to give unto them beauty for ashes, the oil of joy for mourning, the garment of praise for the spirit of heaviness; that they might be called trees of righteousness, the planting of the Lord, that he might be glorified."

God wants things to grow. That's His nature, that's His desire. But no matter how desperate God is for growth, He will never, and I mean never, allow things to grow that won't be cared for. That's a principle you can take to the bank. That's why the Bible says, 'God will turn the wisdom of the wicked into foolishness.' When your so-called wisdom isn't bringing beauty into this world, when it's not aligning with God's purposes, He will flip the script on you. He will take that worldly wisdom and turn it into utter foolishness. So you better check yourself and make sure your wisdom is the kind that brings forth beauty, the kind that aligns with God's heart.

Deborah? woke up, and then she awakened Barak. But it didn't stop there. Barak, in turn, awakened the other fighters. There were people Barak was connected to that Deborah wasn't. She had her connection with Barak, sure, but Barak? He was plugged into those soldiers who had lost their fight, who had given up on their battles.

There are people you're connected to that I'm not. As you wake up to your purpose, as you step into your calling, they're going to wake up too. It's a ripple effect, spreading out far beyond what you can see right now.

When Deborah woke him up, he didn't just roll over and go back to sleep. He said, 'God said go, I will defeat him.' And that's the kind of attitude we need to have. Go capture your enemies, son of Abinoam. Go capture what's been reproaching the body of Christ. It's time to take territory, folks! Go capture the banks, go capture the industries, capture the field, capture the scientific world, capture manufacturing. Lord, capture my name!

It's time to awake and capture your enemies. But here's where it gets interesting. Barak, he had a condition. He said, 'I will not go unless you come with me.' And Deborah? She laid it out straight. She said, 'If I go with you, you will win; if I don't go with you, you will win. Either way, this is your season of winning.'

Because this is important. If you're always waiting for someone else to call and pray for you every day, yeah, you might win, but the victory? It's going to be credited to someone else. But if you go yourself, if you step out in faith, you're going to become a big name. You're going to orchestrate your own standing out.

Deborah, she didn't mince words. She told Barak, 'Because of your attitude - this wrong attitude - you won't be honored with Sisera's defeat. The Lord's going to allow a woman to defeat Sisera instead.' And let me tell you something, women - there are a whole lot of Siseras out there that God has called you to defeat. Men, you're not off the hook either. There are Siseras that God wants you to conquer too. And I'm telling you, this season? You're gonna defeat them.

God didn't call Deborah. No, Deborah responded to an assignment. She saw what needed to be done, and she stepped up. She orchestrated her standing out - she stood out. Just like Joseph. He orchestrated his standing out, and boy, did he ever stand out!

That's what God's looking for. He's looking for people who are willing to take initiative, who are ready to step into their purpose without waiting for a written invitation. He's looking for people who understand His heart, who grasp what He's interested in, and who are willing to align themselves with His purposes.

God's interest? It's in growth, yes, but not just any growth. He's interested in sustainable development that brings forth beauty and life. He's interested in you becoming all He created you to be, in you standing out for His glory. He's interested in you waking up to your purpose and then waking up others around you.

Work, Wisdom, And Discretion

The Lord God looked upon the garden He had created and saw that it was good but not yet complete. For there, flowing through Eden, was a river that would become the source of life and abundance for all that was to come. And the Lord God, knowing the potential within this river, decided to use it as a catalyst for growth and beauty. In verse 9, we see the manifestation of this divine plan, as the Lord God caused all manner of trees to spring forth from the earth - trees that were pleasing to the eye and good for food. But amongst these many trees, two stood out as unique, placed deliberately in the middle of the garden: the tree of life and the tree of knowledge of good and evil.

This river that flowed from Eden, watering the garden and bringing life to all it touched, didn't simply stop there. No, it separated into four smaller rivers, each with its name and purpose. The first of these was called Pishon, a mighty waterway that encircled the entire land of Havilah. And let me tell you, this wasn't just any ordinary land. Havilah was blessed with abundance, particularly in the form of gold - and not just any gold, mind you, but gold of the purest quality. Your time is coming, beloved, when you, too, will experience this abundance. But that's not all - this land was also rich in precious stones and fragrances, all because of the life-giving waters of Pishon.

The second river bore the name Gihon, which had a specific

purpose, flowing around the land of Cush. The third river was called Tigris, making its way eastward of Assyria. Now, I promised to give you a deeper explanation of the meaning behind these rivers another time, so hold onto that thought. Finally, we come to the fourth river, the Euphrates - and let me tell you, this was no ordinary river. The Euphrates was the most powerful of them all, a force to be reckoned with in its own right.

The Lord God put the man in the Garden of Eden to work the soil and care for the garden.' This, my friends, is where we see man's true purpose revealed. On that sixth day of creation, with everything else in place, God decided to shape the course of human history. He decided to rest, but not because He was tired or needed a break. No, God ceased from His work because He had a more excellent plan in mind - He was entrusting the care and cultivation of His creation to man.

This is a truth that holds firm even to this day. Any human being who puts their hand to work will rule, whether they're born again or not. It's as simple as that. The blessing of the Lord rests upon the work of your hands, and whatsoever you do shall prosper. This isn't just some nice saying or motivational quote - it's a fundamental principle of life. A man or woman can orchestrate an outstanding life for themselves by studying their work, giving their all to it, and pouring their best efforts into the task at hand. It's about working the ground of your field, whatever that field may be, and tending to the garden entrusted to you.

I want you to listen closely. Laziness? It's one of the master keys to failure. And let me be clear - God hates it. He can't stand it. He has no patience for cowards, despises those who sow division among the brethren and doesn't accept excuses for unproductivity. When God finds a man or woman who's willing to roll up their sleeves and get to work, connecting with His grace, that's when He causes beautiful things to grow. But here's the catch - not all work is created equal in God's eyes. There are specific things you do that He considers as true work.

So, how do you orchestrate your standing out? How do you position yourself for greatness? Well, let's take a page from Joseph's book, shall we? This young man, he didn't just sit around waiting for someone to make him stand out. No sir! He orchestrated certain things, set certain wheels in motion that would eventually lead him to the palace. Sure, there were some delays along the way - life has a funny way of throwing curveballs at us, doesn't it? But Joseph, he kept working. He honed his skills, interpreting dreams, and when his paycheck finally came? Boy, was it a doozy! He was paid with the throne itself.

So I ask you—what's your work? What's the garden that God is holding back from, refusing to let beautiful things grow in because you've failed to work the ground? It's time for some serious introspection, friends. It's time to roll up those sleeves and get to work.

When Joseph finally stood before Pharaoh, after interpreting that dream that had the ruler of Egypt in an uproar, he didn't just stop there. No, he went a step further. He said, 'Pharaoh, look for a wise and discreet man.' Before making that recommendation, Joseph had worked internally to make himself wise and discreet. He'd put in the hours, so to speak, cultivating those very qualities he was now prescribing. And what was the result? Pharaoh looked at him and said, 'Where can we find such a man? You are the man, as wise and discreet as you are.' Do you see what happened there? Joseph had positioned himself so perfectly that he was the only logical choice when the opportunity arose. This, my friends, is why every investment into becoming wiser is a work that will soon give you a platform that no ruler or king can find someone to substitute you. Every effort you put into developing discretion, knowing how to protect things, safeguarding information - it's all part of the work.

Thieves cannot claim to be discreet. If Esther had not been discreet with the king, she would have died long before Mordecai had the chance to tell her that God put her there for a purpose. Some people's weakness lies in thinking they're trying to be honest, not realizing they're just being foolish—they're not discreet.

Mordecai told Esther. 'Don't tell anyone you're a Jew, Hadassah. Don't tell them your real name.' Some of you might think, 'But I just want to serve God honestly. It's just me being honest.' Listen closely, honey. That's you being honest to Mordecai - and that's all that matters. What you think is honesty can be a trap that will kill you before your time. And when you die, you'll be asking God, 'Why did I die untimely?' The answer? Because you were not discreet.

You start talking to a guy, and you're head over heels in love. Before you know it, all your friends know about him. They've got his number, learn about your past mistakes, and are too happy to share that information. And then, out of the blue, the guy says, 'Sorry, um, the Lord said no.' But let me tell you something - it's not the Lord that said no. It's your friends that said it. Your friends!

Don't get me wrong. Being discreet doesn't mean you hide your truth from your Mordecai. You can say, 'Well, I'm discreet,' but a woman killer you don't even know might look and say, 'Hey, baby, this one - no, this one will kill you. He will suppress you, he will press you at night, he will kill you.' This one - don't trust her. This one - don't trust him. You can trust, but that you are with the king... Do you know that the day came that even for Hadassah to reveal herself, she needed three days of fasting and prayer?

Some of you don't understand how important you are. So, God started something beautiful in your life, and the whole world has known. Before it even reaches any level of maturity, it's dead. Satan killed it on arrival. 'Where can we find a man as wise and discreet?' That's the question we need to be asking ourselves. This season that God is awakening you - this season that God is about to show off with your life - this season that destiny has been waiting for... may the God of Heaven equip you with what it takes to manifest without abortion.

Joseph orchestrated his standing out. Every time God begins to make ways for you, God counts on your discretion and wisdom. This is a season when wisdom and discretion are in high demand. You are a part of something glorious in the house of God, and then the whole world has to know. No, you are not wise—that's not how you do it.

Purpose, Identity, And The Timing Of God

God, in His wisdom, will never - and I mean never - allow a Haman to show up until Esther is adequately prepared. if you're out there, feeling like an Esther, and you hear that Haman is lurking around, trying to wipe out the Jews, don't you dare start thinking, "Well, if these Jewish people were Jewish enough, Haman wouldn't be coming after them." That kind of thinking is dangerous, and it's dead wrong.

Never consider a challenge in the body of Christ, your church, or your family as evidence that God's presence is absent. Sometimes, these challenges prove that God is with you more than you ever imagined. You see when you're in the midst of trouble and crisis, yet you find yourself calm and calculated, that supernatural peace can only come from one source, and that's God Almighty.

I don't know how He does it, but He always makes a way. And let me tell you something else - I don't know how, but you will do it too. You will make a way because the God who lives in you is the Way Maker Himself. God will never allow Haman to flex his muscles until Esther is in position. So, my dear Esther, whoever you are out there, the moment you see Haman screaming and making noise, you better understand that the days of your purpose have arrived. Whatever it costs you, you've got to pay that price. You've got to go deep into the Spirit. You've got to start looking for the solution. That's how you orchestrate your standing out.

You might think you've already stood out by becoming queen and marrying the king. But let me tell you- the purpose of that standout hasn't even begun to be actualized yet. It's not just about marrying a king. If he's a king, where are your babies? It's much more than just being the king's wife.

You've got to say, "God, You didn't give me this kind of access so that I could flex my beauty. You gave me access to reveal Your beauty." And then you've got to believe, with every fiber of your being, that God has been waiting for such a time when a person like you is there to care for what He grows. So you've got to pray, "God, grow Your kingdom through me."

Even Mordecai became a benefactor of Esther's purpose. The man who mentored her, who fathered her, who counseled her - the Bible says he went from being an excellent man to being a great man. Why? Because that time came when God decided that opportunities like this would give people a chance to stand out. So, even if you don't think you're called to stand out, let me set you straight. As a child of God, you must know that God will allow crises and challenges to come your way. Not to break you but to allow you to take advantage of them and stand out.

> Matthew 26:10 (KJV) *"When Jesus understood it,*
> *he said unto them, Why trouble ye the woman? For*
> *she hath wrought a good work upon me."*

A woman broke an expensive oil box and poured it on Jesus while He was still alive. All His disciples, including that traitor Judas Iscariot, said, "What a waste!" But Jesus? He saw something different. He said, "Leave that woman alone. There's nowhere the gospel is preached that her name will not be mentioned." And guess what He said about the woman? He said, "She has done this in preparation for My burial." This woman orchestrated her standing out. She didn't wait for someone to give her permission. She didn't wait for the "right" moment. She seized the opportunity before her and did something so radical and unexpected that Jesus Himself said her name would be remembered forever.

You are about to stand out. You've been waiting on God, and God has been waiting for this time. So now that the time has come, you've got to understand the calendar and marry it to the agenda.

The agenda marrying the calendar - that's what it's all about.

Acts 13:22. This is a commendation from God Himself about David. He says, "I have searched the land and found this David, son of Jesse. He is a man after My own heart." This means David's heart is in sync with God's heart. That's what made David stand out. They ignored, despised, and rejected, but David's strength was his heart, which beat in rhythm with God's heartbeat.

I shared this with the folks in Jos during that mission trip I told you about earlier. It's one of the most powerful things you can do to build a strong relationship. If a woman can, for no reason, put her head on a man's chest, and if that man has a sense of destiny, she can feel his heartbeat. Let me warn you: if he doesn't understand destiny, please don't do it, or stupid things might jump into your head. But if you can put your heart against God's heart? Oh, my friends, He will wake you up in ways others won't understand. He will consume you with Himself.

That's why people won't understand when you, like Paul, say, "I'm willing to spend and be spent. I count all things but dung for the excellency of the knowledge of Christ." They'll think you're crazy, but you'll know you're just in love - in love with a God who's called you to stand out.

If Deborah orchestrated her standing out, and today we read about her - if Joseph and Esther did the same - I'm convinced we will read about you in a few years, even in your lifetime. Your flaws and failures? They're not a threat to God. The only danger God sees is the condition of your heart. What do you love more? Who do you love more? What do you prefer? What will you pay to stand out, especially if you orchestrate it yourself?

Let me tell you what that price might look like. It might be the price of mercy and forgiveness. It might be the price of not giving up on God, even when you want to throw everything in the towel. It might be the price of not giving up on yourself, even when everyone else has. It might be the price of sacrificial living - of pouring yourself out for others even when you feel you have nothing to give.

No fight was left in the warriors until Deborah rose. Deborah became a mother in Israel. Some of you think God wants to make a father, a mother, a dignitary not just within your church but beyond - to the body of Christ, our world, our nation, and our generation. So God asked me to say to you: orchestrate your standing out.

> Esther 2:12-14 (KJV): *"Now when every maid's turn came to go into king Ahasuerus, after that, she had been twelve months according to the manner of the women, for so were the days of their purifications accomplished, to wit, six months with oil of myrrh, and six months with sweet odors, and with other things for the purifying of the women. And thus came every maiden unto the king; whatsoever she desired was given her to go in with her out of the house of the women unto the king's house."*

For one whole year, she was being administered oil. On a typical day, she could have said, "Ahh, I'm tired. Why oil every day? Yesterday's oil is good for tomorrow." But no, she understood the importance of preparation. Every single day until the day came. And when that day came? She was ready.

Adam and Eve were in that perfect paradise for four days—just four days of caring for the garden. On the fourth day of their existence, the serpent slithered in and made them doubt God. "Did God say you shouldn't eat this?" he asked. As soon as he attacked their identity, they began to doubt God's integrity.

That's why God wants me to say to you right now: never doubt who He is to you. Never doubt who you are to Him. You matter to Him more than you can ever imagine. Your identity is not in what you do, have, or what people say about you. Your identity is in who God says you are.

You'll truly stand out when you understand your identity in Christ, grasp His purpose in your life, and align yourself with His perfect timing. That's when you'll become the Esther, the Joseph, the Deborah of your generation.

Don't wait for someone else to make you stand out. Don't wait for the perfect circumstances. Start orchestrating your standing out right now. Dive deep into God's word. Spend time in His presence. Let your heart beat in sync with His. Be ready and prepared, like Esther with her daily oil treatments. Be bold and courageous, like Deborah rallying the troops. Be faithful and persistent, like Joseph, amid his trials. Your time is coming. It might already be here. The question is - are you ready to step into it? Are you prepared to orchestrate your standing out? Because let me tell you, when you do, when you align yourself with God's purpose and timing, there's no limit to what He can do through you. You'll stand out not for your glory but for His. And that, my friends, is what it's all about.

CONCLUSION

I feel blessed to have taken this route with you. We must reminisce on everything we've explored, the lessons, and the truths revealed. This book has walked us through the powerful keys to a lifted life—a life not bound by limitations or held back by obstacles. Through the principles of prophetic warfare, divine alignment, humility, and spiritual battles, we've come to see that living a life of lifting requires more than passive belief. It requires active engagement with the Word of God and a heart ready to align with His purpose.

Everything that the believer needs lies in the power of alignment. Over and over again, we've seen that it's not enough to have faith in God; you must be aligned with His will. In her deep sorrow and barrenness, we saw how Hannah found her breakthrough when she aligned her desires with God's plan for her life. She didn't receive her miracle when weeping at the altar, but when she shifted her heart and recognized that only God could change her situation. It was at that point of alignment that her horn was lifted.

This same principle applies to every area of your life. God's lifting comes when your heart, mind, and actions are aligned with His will. Many times, believers struggle and wonder why their prayers seem unanswered. They may feel stuck or burdened, but what's missing is that crucial element of alignment. It's not enough to cry out to God or to pray for deliverance. You must align your heart with God's will and submit entirely to His plan, and that's where breakthrough happens. Hannah's story is a living example of what happens when we stop fighting for our strength and allow God to lift us according to His purpose.

We also saw the importance of warfare with prophecy. Prophecy is not something to be watched passively. When God speaks a word over your life, it becomes a tool you must use in the spiritual realm. Many people fail to see their prophetic promises come to pass because they sit back and expect them to happen independently. But that's not how God works. Prophecy requires your participation. You don't watch prophecy—you war with prophecy. You fight for the fulfillment of what God has spoken over you.

The story of Zechariah and the four horns that scattered Judah, Israel, and Jerusalem shows us the reality of the spiritual battles we face. Behind every setback, every delay, and every attack, forces are working against you. But God has also prepared artisans to terrify and throw down those horns. The enemy's goal is to scatter and destroy what God wants to build in your life, but God has given you the tools to defeat those powers. He's sent spiritual artisans into your life—through godly mentors, divine interventions, or spiritual revelations—so you can rise above every opposition.

This isn't a passive process. Victory comes to those who are active, vigilant, and ready to fight. You must rise in spiritual warfare, use the prophetic words spoken over your life, and engage in the battle. The enemy will not give up easily, but the promise we have from God is that as long as we remain aligned with Him, no power can stand against us. Victory is assured, but you must claim it, fight for it, and walk in it.

Equally important is the rejection of witchcraft and rebellion. These two forces have held many believers down for far too long. Often, when we think of witchcraft, we imagine spells and curses, but the reality is that rebellion against God's Word is itself a form of witchcraft. The Bible clearly states that rebellion is the sin of witchcraft. We saw how Saul fell into rebellion despite his anointing and calling. He disobeyed God's clear instructions and ended up consulting a witch, which ultimately led to his downfall.

This teaches us a powerful lesson: rebellion blocks your lifting. When you reject God's Word or refuse to submit to His will, you open the door for demonic forces to influence your life. Saul's story is a warning to all of us. God desires to lift you, but your heart must be fully submitted. Pride, stubbornness, and rebellion will only lead to destruction, as we saw in Saul's case. But when you humble yourself, align with God's will, and walk in obedience, nothing can stop you from lifting.

Humility is not just a good trait but the key to sustained lifting. Many people experience breakthrough moments but fail to maintain that lifting because they let pride slip in. As soon as they experience some success, they forget where God brought them from and begin to rely on their strength. But God resists the proud and gives grace to the humble. The lifting that comes from God is not meant to be temporary. He desires to establish and set you on solid ground, but that only happens when you remain humble and entirely dependent on Him.

Psalm 125:1 says, **"Those who trust in the Lord are as unshakeable as Mount Zion."** When God lifts you, He doesn't lift you just to see you fall again. His lifting is meant to be a permanent shift, but it's up to you to align with Him. This means continually walking in humility, recognizing that everything you have and everything you are comes from Him. The moment you begin to think you can do it on your own is the moment you start to lose that lifting.

We explained thoroughly the importance of spiritual discernment. You must discern the difference between what lifts and what pulls down as God lifts you. Not everything that looks good is from God, and not every opportunity is meant to be taken. Spiritual discernment is the ability to see beyond the surface and recognize what aligns with God's purpose for your life. As

God elevates you, there will be many distractions, temptations, and even people sent by the enemy to pull you down. But with discernment, you can navigate these challenges and stay focused on your God-given assignment.

To finish, this journey has been a call to radical surrender. Surrendering to God is not a one-time decision but a daily posture of the heart. It's easy to say, "Lord, have Your way," but genuinely allowing God to take control of every aspect of your life requires a deep level of trust. You must be willing to lay down your plans, desires, and expectations and trust that God's plan for your life is far greater than anything you could ever imagine.

Surrender is the key to unlocking God's glory in your life. When you fully yield to Him, you open the door for His supernatural power to work in ways that go beyond your natural abilities. God's glory is the ultimate lifting force. It's not about what you can achieve alone but what God can do through you when you give Him complete control.

As you close this book, I want you to remember that the lifting God has planned for your life is not temporary, nor do your circumstances limit it. No matter where you are right now or how many obstacles you face, God's power is available to lift you higher. But you must remain aligned, stay in warfare, reject rebellion, and walk humbly. These are the keys to experiencing God's lifting and sustaining it.

You are called to greatness, and with God's help, you will rise above every limitation. This is your season to be lifted but requires your full participation. Don't let the enemy steal what God has declared over your life. Fight for it, align with His will, and trust that the God who lifted you will keep you lifted. No power can stop you from fulfilling your divine destiny with God on your side.

A SPECIAL CALL TO SALVATION & NEW BEGINNINGS FROM APOSTLE DR. DAVID PHILEMON

Dear Beloved,

God loves you deeply and has brought you to this moment for a reason. No matter your past, His love and forgiveness are available to you.

The Bible says in John 3:16, "For God so loved the world that He gave His one and only Son, that whoever believes in Him shall not perish but have eternal life." Jesus Christ came to save you, offering you a new life of purpose and peace.

If you're ready to accept Jesus as your Lord and Savior, pray this simple prayer:

The Salvation Prayer

"Heavenly Father, I come to You in the Name of Jesus. I acknowledge that I am a sinner in need of a Savior. I believe that Jesus Christ is Your Son, that He died for my sins, and that You raised Him from the dead. I repent of my sins and turn to You with my

Whole heart. Jesus, I ask You to come into my life. Be my Lord and my Savior. I surrender my life to You. Fill me with Your Holy Spirit, guide me on the path of righteousness, and help me to follow Your script for my life. Thank you, Father, for saving me. In the name of Jesus. Amen."

Welcome to the Family of God!

If you have just prayed this prayer, Congratulations! You are now a child of God, and heaven is rejoicing. Your journey has begun, and we're here to support you as you grow in faith and discover God's unique plans for you.

Next Steps:
- Connect with a Bible-believing church.
- Read the Bible Daily: God's Word is your guide.
- Pray Regularly: Prayer is your lifeline to God.
- Share Your Faith: Don't keep the good news to yourself.

.

www.ingramcontent.com/pod-product-compliance
Lightning Source LLC
Chambersburg PA
CBHW071905020426
42331CB00010B/2674